PALLAVA ANTIQUITIES

PALLAVA ANTIQUITIES

G. JOUVEAU-DUBREUIL

TRANSLATED INTO ENGLISH BY

V.S. SWAMINADHA DIKSHITAR

IN TWO VOLUMES
Vol. I

(With 32 Plates)

Published by

Facsimile Publisher
12 Pragati Market
Ashok Vihar, Ph-2
Delhi-110052
facsimilepublisher.com

Distribution Network
gyanbooks.com
India, USA, Canada, UK, Australia, France

ISBN : 978-93-5324-413-2 (Set)
ISBN : 978-93-5324-414-9 Vol. 1 (HB)
First Published, London, 1916

2nd Impression 2020

Printed at: Gyan Press, Delhi.

Pallava Antiquities
Author: G. Jouveau-Dubreuil

PALLAVA ANTIQUITIES.

BY

G. JOUVEAU-DUBREUIL,

Doctor of the University of Paris.
Professor, College. Pondicherry.

VOL. I.

(*With 32 Plates*)

LONDON:

PROBSTHAIN AND CO.,
41, Great Russell Street.

1916

PREFACE.

In presenting Volume I of "Pallava Antiquities" to the public, the author wishes it to be known that this is the first of a series of volumes which he hopes to publish by continuing his researches and making new discoveries concerning the Pallavas.

The subject-matter of this book is a study of the Antiquities already discovered but which have not been thoroughly studied.

The author has confined himself to a comparison of the Pallava monuments with one another; he has not, therefore, attempted to compare the monuments of the Pallava period with those of other periods with a view to determine the distinctive characters of the Pallava Art.

In fact, this subject has been already treated in his work "Archéologie du Sud de l'Inde, Paris, 1914", but as this book is written in French and is thus not within reach of all readers in India, he has written in English an epitome of it, a booklet called "Dravidian Architecture" in which he has specially examined the characters which distinguish the Pallava monuments from those of other epochs. Besides, he has also ascertained and fixed the technical terms that must be used in designating the different parts of a building.

This epitome, which, in the author's opinion, is indispensable for the study of Pallava Art, is actually in the press and will appear before the end of the current year.

The original of "Pallava Antiquities, Vol. I" was written in French during the month of June 1916. (*Vide* "Revue Historique de l'Inde Française" in which it has been published under the heading "Les Antiquités de l'époque Pallava" in Vol. I, 1st half-year of 1916, 34, Galerie d'Orléans, Paris).

The present work is a translation of it made in July 1916 by M. R. Ry. V. S. Swaminadha Dikshitar B.A., L.T., officier d'académie, Professor of English in the Colonial College, Pondicherry, to whom the author tenders his hearty thanks.

He desires also to thank M. R. Ry. S. Krishnaswami Aiyangar, the learned Professor of History and Archæology in the University of Madras, for his having kindly given tentative translations of the Panamalai, and Mêlachêri inscriptions.

PONDICHERRY,
August 1916.

G. J-D.

INTRODUCTION.

The traveller who formerly took the road from Pondicherry to Madras, found on his way very strange monuments: these were not built of stones placed above one another, but were simply rocks that the sculptor's chisel had worked on, either to give them the external form of a building, or to excavate in them subterranean chambers.

Being situated near Madras, these curious pieces of sculpture that fittingly attract the attention of archæologists have been variously described under the name of "the antiquities of Mahābalipuram" or "the Seven Pagodas"[1]

It must however be mentioned that these monuments are interesting, not so much because they are cut in the rock, but because these sculptures are so very beautiful.

The rock-cut temples at Mahābalipuram are sculptured in an elegant architectural style: the capitals, the brackets, the cornices, the roofs, the gable-ends, have the most graceful forms and are ornamented with rose-work, foliage and volute which produce a most charming effect.

This is not all: the numerous bas-reliefs represent personages whose beautiful attitudes and poses compel admiration. Very often these personages have a calm and peaceful attitude: their gestes are full of

1. Concerning a description of the "Seven Pagodas," *Vide* "Archéologie du Sud de l'Inde" vol. I, pp. 75-102.

sweetness and serenity ; but the bas-reliefs that represent scenes of violence are full of life. As an example I will mention the justly celebrated bas-relief of the fight between Kâḷî and the giant Mahishâsura, which is assuredly one of the best works in India.

The sculpture is the visible manifestation of intellectual progress: and it is certain that the sculptors of Mahabalipuram had attained a high degree of civilisation.

Who were these men and when did they live? There is no doubt that the Hindu princes who reigned over this part of India when those rocks were carved belonged to the Pallava dynasty.

The monuments in the Seven-Pagodas contain in fact inscriptions in praise of the Pallava princes. Besides, in many other places, at Kâñchîpuram, Śīyamaṅgalam, Trichinopoly, etc., there are found some temples similar to those of Mahābalipuram and containing Pallava inscriptions.

The temples at Mahābalipuram, as well as all those that have been discovered in other places and contain similar inscriptions, can therefore be considered as the work of the Pallavas.

Luckily, the history of the Pallavas is known to us otherwise than by the inscriptions engraved on the monuments. Numerous documents have been discovered which are written on copper-plates and give us precious information on the subject.

The question now is this: given a Pallava temple, to which king of that dynasty are we to attribute it? This interesting question has led to many researches. We may affirm, however, that this problem has not so far been solved in a satisfactory manner.

The only method that has been followed to discover the age of these Pallava monuments is the study of the inscriptions found on them. This study is certainly necessary: but it is a mistake to believe that that alone is sufficient. However, the present-day opinion is that the study of these inscriptions is the only means of arriving at a solution.

Mr. E. Hultzch, in a recent work on this question (Epigraphia Indica, Vol. X, No. 1, page 1: The Pallava inscriptions of the Seven Pagodas), has written:

« The important question of the authors and the » dates of those excavations can be answered *only* by a » careful study of the inscriptions engraved on them. »

Why, this method of investigation will not do: if employed all alone, great mistakes may be committed. It is possible that the inscriptions on a monument have been written long after it was erected, and then these inscriptions not only do they not give us any information about the author, but may even lead us into error.

An important factor in determining the age of a monument, is the study of the style of the sculptures. This important element has been totally neglected up to the present.

It will be very useful to find out exactly the style of the rock-cut temples of Mahêndravâḍi, Vallam, Dalavânûr, Pallâvaram, etc. But then it is remarkable that up to the present time the photographs of these monuments have not been reproduced in any work.

We should therefore study the styles of all the monuments which could be attributed to the Pallavas. For that purpose, we have visited all the places where this kind of monuments and inscriptions were reported to exist; nay more, we have tried to discover others, and very often our efforts have been crowned with success. Notably at Panamalai and at Mêlachêri, we have luckily discovered certain temples and inscriptions a knowledge of which has supplied new elements for the history of the antiquities of this kind.

We wish then to make a general study of it; for this we must compare the monuments from three different standpoints:

1° the tenor of the inscriptions;

2° the form of the letters in which the inscriptions are written;

3° the style of the sculptures.

It is the result of these researches that we give below.

In many cases, we shall have occasion to propound new ideas; in many others, our conclusions may not be very different from those arrived at by others; however, even in the latter case, we think that this study shall not have been useless, for these ideas will appear to be more correct, being based on a greater number of proofs.

CHAPTER I.

THE EPOCH OF RÂJASIMHA.

In the "South Indian Inscriptions" by Mr. E. Hultzsch (Madras 1890) No. 31, page 24, a question is raised concerning a cave-temple at Panamalai[1] which contains an inscription consisting of a single Sanskrit verse which is identical with the last verse of the principal inscription in the Kaïlâsanâtha temple at Kâñchîpuram. The fac-simile of this inscription has been communicated to Mr. Hultzsch by M. R. Ry. Râghavendrâchârya of Vânûr.

From the translation of this Sanskrit verse, Mr. Hultzsch has concluded that the cave at Panamalai was cut by Râjasiṁha, the prince who had built the Kailâsanâtha temple at Kâñchîpuram.

On the 1st January 1915, I went to Panamalai with the object of photographing this cave, and as it contained an inscription of Râjasiṁha, I wished to know the style of a temple cut in the rock during his time.

Having arrived on the spot, I saw the inscription mentioned above, but I found that it was not written in a temple cut in the rock, but simply on an anfractuosity of the rock within which an image of Kâli (Mahishâsuramardani) has been placed.

1. Panamalai is a village in the Villupuram Taluk (South Arcot District)—(See Madras list of Antiquities by Sewell, Vol. 1, page 209, and Madras District Gazetteers—"South Arcot" by Francis (1906) page 385.)

This small natúral cavern is situated at the foot of a rock. At its top is a small temple which I visited.

Standing before the temple, I ascertaind two things: 1° that the style of the temple is the same as that of the Kailâsanâtha temple at Kâñchîpuram; 2° that round the base of this temple is engraved in a single line an inscription written in that characteristic alphabet known as the " Grantha-Pallava."

This inscription is not mentioned anywhere. M.R.Ry. H. Krishna Sastri, Government Epigraphist for South India, to whom I communicated it, was good enough to write to me on the 27th August 1915: « In ac-
» knowledging with thanks your printed note on the
» Pallava inscription at Panamalai, forwarded with
» your letter of the 20th instant, I beg to inform you
» that the inscription you have discovered is a new one.
» It has been neither published nor even noticed hiterto.»

The discovery of a temple, the architectural style of which is the same as that of the Kailâsanâtha temple at Kâñchîpuram and which contains an inscription, enables us now to have new documents for the history of Pallava antiquities.

We shall therefore study:

1° the tenor of the inscription;

2° the style of the temple;

3° the form of the letters of the alphabet used in the inscription.

Section I. The tenor of the inscription.

The beginning and the end of the inscription are concealed by a structure of bricks built in front of the temple. So a portion of the first sentence and the whole of the last part of the inscription are missing. The letters have been preserved excellently well except towards the middle wherefrom a stone which contained some letters has been removed.

I published in July 1915 a tentative translation of it. As this seemed to be insufficient, M. R. Ry. S. Krishnaswami Aiyangar, Professor in the University of Madras, has been pleased to give me a more correct translation of the inscription from my reproduction of it. (*Plate I*).

Text:

(U)dapādi prathita bhuja balo Drōṇi[1] raṁśaḥ Purārēḥ
(Drōṇi na)mnōtha tasmāṅnicita gurutapō nimma-
lādāvirāsîdāmnayadanga vidyā visara iva Mahīvalla
(bho Pall-)vākyaḥ
Yasmādeṣaḥ ... pathivihita padād pāvanē[2] mānanīyō
mandākinyā(ḥ) pravā-
haḥ Śaśina iva Mahānanvayaḥ Pallavānāmsaṁrājama-
śvamē
dhāvabhṛ(ta) virajasām bhūbhuj(ām) Pallavānāṁ
addhṛ...
ṣṭā Pallavānāvimalatara bharadvājavaṁśōdbhavānām
kētō
rakṣīṇabāhu draviṇa hṛta mahī cakra vikhyāta kīrtēr
yyō devā......
dēkamallād Guha iva Para..........bhujadraviṇāva bhāsi
satvō-
rjjitam samaradṛpta Mahaprabhava[3] Yō Rājasimha iti
viśru-
ta puṇyakīrti rudṛtta śatru nṛpa Kunjararājasimhaḥ
hartādvi-

1. *Drounih*, the son or descendant of Drōna.—(*S.K.*)
2. *pāvanō* seems the correct form.—(*S.K.*)
3. may also be read *subhava*.—(*S.K.*)

ṣadvargga samuccrayāṇām kartāca Kalyāna parampa rāṇām
cittē sadā sabhrta [1] bhakti pūtē dhattē sadā...
...Yasya (mṛ)gā(ṅ)ka mōḷi [2] ... tē sala kusuma kṛtakānti malaṁca
Manāḥ sadvṛttāpēna sēkai(ḥ) druma iva sata (ḥ) (ṁ)ca taptōsi darmma.

Tentative Translation.

Drōṇi [3] famed for the might of his arm was born a (minor) incarnation of Śiva.

From him of the name Drôṇi, pure by the performance of great penance, there appeared, as the sciences of the Vedanga from the Veda, the ruler of the earth named Pallava

From whom (did descend), as the floods of the Ganges from the moon, [4] the great family of the Pallavas, sanctified by treading in the path (of righteousness), holy and so worthy of great esteem.

A dynasty of paramount soverigns, made pure by the frequent baths at the conclusion of the (numerous) horse-sacrifices [5] performed by them.

1. may be '*Sadhrta*'—(*S. K.*)
2. *mauli* is the correct form.—(*S. K.*)
3. Drōnih, or more correctly Drauni, was son of Drōna the preceptor of the Pandava and Kaurava Princes. The Pallavas claim descent from him by a Nāga Princess. Slokas 4 and 5 of *S. I. I.*, Vol. I., Ins 32.—(*S. K.*)
4. There is nothing, so far as I know, to connect the Ganges and the moon in this manner unless it be a reference to the Ganges flowing from the matted locks of Siva where also resides the crescent moon.—(*S. K.*)
5. Horse-sacrifices are performed to assert one's claims to the position of King of Kings or Emperor. The great-sacrifice, like other sacrifices, concludes with a bath which is considered peculiarly holy, as bringing to a conclusion a work of great merit.—(*S. K*)

The chief of this family, the like of which did not exist before, and which belonged to the most holy tribe (gotra) of Bhāradvāja ;[1]

Whose fame had spread over the circle of the world which was taken forcible possession of (conquered) by the undiminished prowess of his arm ;

Who, (born) from him (who bore) the title Ēkamalla,[2] as Guha (Subrahmanya) from God Paramēśvara,[3] shone with the prowess of his arm ;

Who was known by the name Rājasiṁha of sanctified reputation, radiant in war-like pride made firm by his own strength ;

Who was king of lions by the destruction of the elephants, the enemy kings ;

Who was destroyer of the crowd of hostile kings and maker of all things auspicious ;

His mind purified by the unremitting hold of devotion (to God), having given always.

. . . .

To whom of Śiva of the deer-spotted (moon) crest.......

The remaining two lines are too far broken up to make any sense as they stand. The inscription does not appear to come to an end.[4]

S. Krishnaswami Aiyangar.

1. Bharadvāja is a Vedic Rishi, considered the progenitor of those that claim to belong to the gōtra of Bharadvāja. Drōnāchārya, and Asvathāma his son, naturally belonged to this Gōtra.—(*S.K.*)

2. This appears to have been a title of Paramesvara I.—(*S.K.*)

3. This seems to imply a reference to the fact that Rājasimha's father also bore the name Paramēsvara. (*Vide* stanza 5, *S. I. I.*, Vol. I., No. 24.)—(*S. K.*)

4. Rājasimha, the "king of lions, destroyer of the elephants, the

The Panamalai inscription greatly resembles the one found at the base of the Vimâna of the Kailâsanâtha temple at Kâñchîpuram (*South Indian Inscriptions*. Vol. I, p. 12, No. 24). Both inscriptions begin with the genealogy of Pallava, the founder of the dynasty.

Then comes a eulogy of the Pallava princes.

Afterwards it is said that in this family was born a prince called Râjasiṁha who was begotten exactly as Paramêśvara begot Guha (Subramaṇya.)

This is not a mere comparison. It means precisely that Râjasiṁha is the son of a King named Paramêśvara.

Then follows a panegyric of Râjasiṁha, who is compared in both the inscriptions to a lion, vanquisher of the elephants, which represent the enemy princes. (According to tradition, the lion is the natural enemy of the elephants.)

hostile kings", was the son and successor of Paramêsvara Varman I, who, according to this inscription, seems to have had the special title "Ekamalla" (the sole warrior). This is exactly to the same purport as Sloka 5 of No. 24 of Vol. I, South Indian Inscriptions,—another inscription of Rājasimha. This seems the first record which gives this title to Paramēsvara Varman I.

The genealogical information that is available in this is Drauni (Asvattāma), his son Pallava, in this line Rājasimha from Paramēsvara Varman I. The other inscription from Panamalai already referred to, containing no more than the Mangala sloka (benedictory verse) of the Kailāsanātha inscription of Rājasimha, this inscription and that taken together indicate that Rājasimha was the builder of the temple at Panamalai, the architectural similarity of which to the shore-temple at Mahābalipûr and to the Kailāsanātha temple at Conjeevaram is already adverted to. In regard to genealogical details as far as they go, and the relation between Paramēsvara and Rājasimha, there is a very close similarity even of expression between this inscription on the one hand, and No. 24 of Vol. I, *S. I. I.*, and the Kasakudi-plates on the other, leaving no doubt that Rājasimha was the son and successor of Paramēsvara Varman I. Rājasimha was a Saiva according to No. 24 referred to above.—(*S.K.*)

Rajasiṁha is called the King of Lions.

What makes it difficult to determine the age of the monuments with the aid of the inscriptions on them is that many Pallava princes have not only the same name, but also the same epithets, which makes it impossible to know exactly which prince is referred to.

But, here, there is no room for doubt, for, there is only one Pallava king, Narasiṁhavarman II, who had the characteristic surname of Râjasiṁha. The inscription on the pillar in Vyâghrapurîśvara temple at Vâyalûr (*vide G. O.* No. 538, 28th July 1909, p. 41, No. 368) contains a complete genealogy of this prince surnamed Râjasiṁha (King of lions) (*G. O.*, No. 538, 28th July 1909, p. 78).

Narasiṁhavarman II was the son of Paramêśvaravarman I; the Panamalai inscription says that very clearly, when comparing his birth to that of Guha; the one being the son of God Paramêśvara and the other the son of the king of the same name.

In his report on the tenor of the Vêlûrpāḷayam plates (*G. O.* No. 832, 28th July 1911, Part II, page 61), M.R.Ry. H. Krishna Sastri says :—

« There is one point of peculiar interest to notice in » this part of the account, viz., the omission of Ma» hêndravarman II after Narasiṁhavarman I, as given » in the accepted genealogy of the Pallavas, and the » suggestion of an unnamed king between Paramêśvara» varman I and Narasiṁhavarman II, the latter being » called the son's son (putra-sûnu) of the former.»

The only explanation that can be given is certainly this :-that the author of the Vêlûrpāḷayam plates did not know well the relationship of the princes that reigned more than one century before the time when he wrote.

The building of Kailâsanâtha temple at Kâñchîpuram was considered as one of the most important events in the reign of Narasiṁhavarman II, for, we find it mentioned in the Vêlûrpāḷayam plates (*G. O.* 28th July 1911, p. 61). In fact, it is said there, that this king built "a stone temple for Śiva resembling Kailāsa."

Besides, this king, according to the plates of Kâsakûdi (*S. I. I.*, Vol. II, part III, p. 342), of Udayendiram (*S. I. I.* Vol. II, part III, p. 371), and of Vêlûrpāḷayam (*G. O.*, 28th July 1911, p. 61), does not seem to have done anything else during his reign except adoring Siva, loading the Brahmans with favours and building temples.

It being granted that this king reigned at the epoch intervening between the victory of Paramêśvaravarman I. over Vikramâditya I. (655-680) and the victory of Vikramāditya II. over Nandivarman - Pallavamalla (about 740), it must be admitted that the temple of Panamalai and that of Kailâsanâtha at Kâñchîpuram have been constructed by Rājasiṁha in the first years of the 8th century (700 to 710 A.D.).

Section II. The style of the temple.

We have then at present two monuments which, judging from the inscriptions on them, appear to be contemporaneous. We have said that they have been built in the same style. It is this that we must now prove by giving an exact description of that style.

As for the temple of Kailâsanâtha at Kâñchîpuram we refer the reader to two works: 1° *Pallava Architecture*, by Alexander Rea, Madras, 1909, in which are given the plan of the temple and some excellent pictures; 2° *Archéologie du Sud de l'Inde*, Volume I,

Architecture, Geuthner Publisher, Paris 1915, pages 103 to 111—a work in which we have tried, for the first time, to define the style of Rajâsiṁhâ. We shall specially describe here the temple of Panamalai :—

1° The plan of the temple presents a very rare peculiarity which is also found in the temple of Kailāsanâtha at Kâñchîpuram (see *Pl. IV*). By the four sides of the sanctuary are placed collateral niches which open either towards the east or towards the west (but never towards north or south). These niches contain Liṅgams.

2° All the Liṅgams at the Panamalai as well as the Kâñchîpuram temple have a peculiar and characteristic form. Whereas the ordinary liṅgam is always cylindrical, here it is in the form of a prism with 8 or 16 faces, (*Pl. VI*). Often these faces are slightly fluted.

3° The sanctuary (Garbhagriham) of the Hindu temples is never ornamented in the interior; the walls around the liṅgam are bare, but at Panamalai and at Kâñchîpuram the walls at the back of the sanctuary are ornamented with an image in bas-relief that represents Sōmaskanda, that is to say, Śiva and Pārvatī with the latter holding the infant Skanda on her lap. On both sides of Śiva, but behind, stand Brahmā and Vishṇu.

4° We find rearing lions supporting the pillars which are at the corners of the edifice. These lions are big and differ much from those that are seen so often in modern temples. The rearing lions as those of Panamalai are seen in large numbers in the Kailâsanâtha temple at Kâñchîpuram.

5° The walls of the temple at Panamalai are adorned with niches, the framework of which has a very special form which is seen often in the temple of Kailâsanâtha at Kâñchîpuram.

We shall give to this framework the name of "Tiruvatchi," as in these days there exists a similar ornament bearing this name.

The Tiruvatchi at Panamalai is formed of a single arch the extremities of which emerge from the mouth of two fabulous animals (Makaras). They have the trunk of an elephant, the tail of foliage, and on these animals are mounted little Gandharvas.

Pl. V. represents this ornamentation of the temples of Râjasiṁha which we shall call "single-arched tiruvatchi."

Upon the whole, by their plan, by their prismatic liṅgams, by the very special image of Sōmaskanda, by their rearing lions and by the single-arched Tiruvatchi, the temples of the epoch of Râjasiṁha can be clearly made out.

Pl. II. will give an idea of the general aspect of the temple at Panamalai.

However, as the details cannot be distinguished, the different parts of the edifice will be found represented in *Pl. III.*

We shall finish by saying that the temples at Panamalai and Kâñchîpuram are not monolithic but are built of blocks of stone superposed on one another.

Section III. The Alphabets of the inscriptions.

We have proved, relying on the tenor of the inscriptions and the style of the monuments, that the temple of Kailâsanâtha at Kâñchîpuram and that at Panamalai are contemporaneous. But, if we compare the letters of the two inscriptions, we see easily that they differ almost entirely from each other.

Plate I.

(PANAMALAI.)

Pallava inscription at Panamalai.

Plate II.

(PANAMALAI.)

Pallava temple at Panamalai (northern side.)

A look at *Pl. VII.* is enough to prove it. On examining them closely, we observe that these letters differ in two ways:

1° The letters of the Kâñchîpuram inscription are florid; in place of straight lines, we find zigzag lines forming various flourishes; the letters of Panamalai are simple.

2° The characters of these two inscriptions are not of the same degree of evolution. The Káñchîpuram alphabet would appear to be about 50 years older. Particularly the letters ग, ज, ण, न, ब, भ, श, स are more archaic.

Since we cannot doubt that the two inscriptions are contemporaneous, we must admit that the form of the characters is not enough to enable us to affirm that one inscription is older than another. However, that is what has been done up to the present.

The Kâñchîpuram inscription that we have mentioned above is the one which is at the base of the sanctuary of Râjasiṁhêśvara in the temple of Kailâsanâtha and which has been translated and published in *South Indian Inscriptions*, Vol. I, p. 12, under No. 24.

There exist in the same temple inscriptions (Nos. 25 and 26) written on the lower part of the sanctuaries (Rathas) that are all round the enclosure of the temple.

The inscriptions are written in four tiers. And each of these is written in a different alphabet. Particularly, the second tier is written in the same alphabet as that of Panamalai. The third tier is in the same florid characters as those of inscription No. 24, which stands at the base of Râjasiṁhêsvara temple. It is therefore certain that these two tiers are contemporaneous.

Relying only on the form of the letters, Mr. E. Hultzsch has affirmed that the third tier belongs to the time of Râjasiṁha but that the second tier must be a later copy made by a successor of Râjasiṁha ;

« ...the third tier is written in the same arcahic alpha-» bet, as the inscription round the Rajasiṁheśvara temple » and evidently belongs to the time of Râjasiṁha, the » founder of the temple, himself. Thus the first and » second tiers must be considered as later copies of the » original inscription in the third tier, which were » executed by some descendants of Râjasiṁha (*S. I. I.*, » Vol. I, p. 10).»

We have not up to this time said anything about the first and the fourth lines. They are written in the same alphabet and it differs entirely from the alphabets we have already spoken of. Whereas the latter are of the Grantha family, the former is of the Nâgarî family. It is certainly a foreign alphabet. At what period were the first and the fourth tiers written ? As the second and third tiers are of the time of Râjasiṁha, it is extremely probable that the first and the fourth lines are contemporaneous with the two others, that is to say, that the four tiers have been written at the time of the construction of the temple by Râjasiṁha.

This opinion is at variance with that of Mr. Hultzsch who says (*Ep. Ind.*, Vol. X, No. 1, p. 3) :

« We may place the inscriptions written in both » alphabets in the time immediatly preceding the con-» quest of the Pallava territory by Vikramaditya II » (A.D. 733-734) to (746-747).»

Mr. Hultzsch is therefore of opinion that these different alphabets are not contemporaneous : only the florid characters are of the time of Râjasiṁha, and the

Plate III.

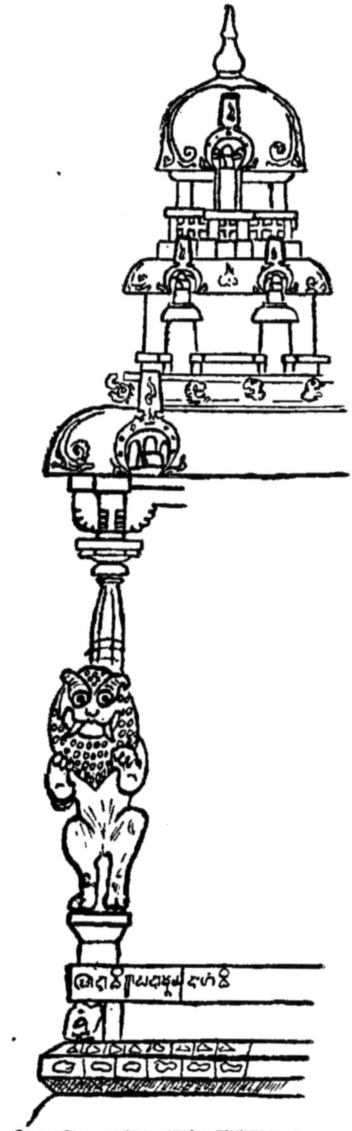

Architectural order of the Pallava temple at Panamalai.

Plate IV.

A. Map of the temple at Panamalai.

B. Map of the garbhagriham of the Kailâsanâtha temple at Kâñchîpuram.

others of that of the successors of this prince, Parameśvaravarman II and Nandivarman-Pallavamalla.

The discovery of the inscription in the temple of Panamalai has proved, on the contrary, that at the time of Râjasiṁha, different kinds of alphabets were used and that a difference in the stage of evolution of the letters does not at all indicate a difference in the ages.

To sum up: it can be affirmed, that, at the time of Narasiṁhavarman II, they used for inscriptions on stones three kinds of Sanskrit alphabets:

1° "The simple Grantha-Pallava" (that of Panamalai). It resembled much the alphabet that was employed in writing on copper plates. (*Vide* inscriptions of Kûram and Kasakûdi.)

2° The florid Grantha-Pallava which is more archaic than the first. This alphabet was perhaps devised by the predecessor of Rajâsiṁha 50 years earlier. As it was much embellished and little employed, it was handed down without any change, and the sculptors of the time of Râjasiṁha who wished to employ this alphabet were satisfied with copying the old models instead of embellishing the writing of their days.

3° The Nâgarî-Pallava alphabet which probably originated in a region of India farther north.

We shall conclude by expressing this new idea that different kinds of alphabets have been able to exist at the same time and that we must not rely only on the degree of evolution of the letters for determining the age.

CHAPTER II.

THE EPOCH OF MAHÊNDRA.

In 1890, M. Hultzsch, in giving a translation of two inscriptions (*S. I. I.*, Vol. I, p. 29. Nos. 33 and 34), has said that the upper cave at Trichinopoly bears the inscriptions of a Pallava king named Guṇabhara surnamed Śatrumalla.

In 1892 (*G. O.* No. 642-3, 14th Aug. 1893—inscription No. 185 of 1892) an inscription of a king named Lalitâṅkura, Śatrumalla, Guṇabhara, Mahêndra-pôtarâja, was discovered at Vallam. V. Venkayya (*Ep .Ind.* Vol. III, p. 277), relying upon Periyapurâṇam, has proved that Śiruttoṇda-Nâyanâr was a contemporary of Narasiṁhavarman I. and that Appar, who was older, was first persecuted and then protected by a king whose surname was Guṇabhara and who must therefore be Mahêndravarman I.

From that he concludes that the caves at Trichinopoly and Vallam must be attributed to the same prince.

In 1896, was discovered (*G. O.* No. 814 - 815, of the 6th August 1896) the inscription (No. 13 of 1896) in the rock-cut temple at Mahêndravâḍi which was dedicated to Vishṇu by King Guṇabhara under the name of Mahêndra-Vishṇugṛiha (*Ep. Ind.*, Vol. IV, p. 153).

In 1900 (*G. O.* Nos. 833-835 of 22nd August 1900) the inscription (No. 67 of 1900) found in the cave at Śîyamaṅgalam which contains the name of a king called Lalitâṅkura (*Ep. Ind.*, Vol. VI, p. 320, No. 32) was, as that of Mahêndravâḍi, attributed to Mahêndravarman I.

In 1905, V. Venkayya attributed to the same king the cave at Dalavânûr (*G. O.* No. 518, 18th July 1905, p. 47) which contains an inscription of Satru-malla (No. 51 of 1905).

Again, in 1909 (*G. O.* No. 538, 28th July 1909, p. 75) M. R. Ry. H. Krishna Sastri attributed also to Mahêndravarman I. the cave of Pallâvaram which bears inscriptions containing the names of kings analogous to those found in the abovementioned caves.

It was thus admitted that the caves and inscriptions at Trichinopoly, Vallam, Mahêndravâḍi, Śîyamaṅgalam, Dalavânûr and Pallâvaram, were contemporaneous and that they must be attributed to Mahêndravarman I.

Now, when Mr. Hultzsch's article on Pallava inscriptions of the Seven Pagodas appeared (*Ind. Ant.*, Vol. X, No. 1), we read in page 2, note 2, this remark:

« The alphabet of the Trichinopoly cave inscription » is more recent, and the opinion that it belongs to » Mahêndravarman I. (*S. I. I.*, Vol. II, p. 341) cannot be » upheld.»

It is true that the inscriptions at Trichinopoly are not written in the same alphabet as those at Dalavânûr, Śîyamaṅgalam and Mahêndravâḍi. During a visit to Trichinopoly, I ascertained that all the inscriptions attributed to Mahêndra, the published ones as well as those that have not yet been published, were written in an alphabet which seems to be more recent than that used at Dalavânûr, Śîyamaṅgalam and Mahêndravâḍi.

Besides, during a visit made to Pallâvaram, I verified the fact already stated by M. R. Ry. H. Krishna Sastri that the Pallâvaram inscriptions were like those at Trichinopoly.

« The inscription in ancient Pallava - Grantha » characters written on the beams of the upper and lower » verandahs of this cave, consists of a single long line of » writing like the one on the pillar in the upper cave » of the Trichinopoly rock. » (*G. O.* 28th July 1909, » page 75).

Thus, from a paleographical point of view, the six caves in question must be divided into 3 categories :

1° The Vallam cave, where the inscription is in the Tamil Alphabet and which therefore is beside the question.

2° The caves at Dalavânûr, Śîyamaṅgalam and Mahêndravâḍi, where the inscriptions are written in a very archaic Grantha-Pallava alphabet.

3° The caves at Trichinopoly and Pallâvaram, where the inscriptions are written in a less archaic and more developed form of Grantha-Pallava characters.

The whole question deserves to be examined anew. The question is : to which kings must these antiquities be attributed and what is their date ?

We think that it is possible to arrive at a solution only by an attentive study of the monuments themselves.

1° From an architectural point of view, nothing has been done ; it is therefore essential to determine the style of these monuments with the aid of photographs of each of them.

2° From a palæographic point of view, the inscriptions which have never been reproduced or have been reproduced but are not enough to give an idea of the exact form of the alphabet, must be examined on the spot.

3° Lastly, it is not useless to know the position of the

Plate V.

Tiruvatchi with a single curvature at Panamalai.

Plate VI.

A
Image of Sômâskanda.

B
Prismatic lingam.

Inner view of the sanctuary at Panamalai.

inscriptions on the monuments. We have therefore studied the monuments on the spot with attention, and we have taken "estampages" and photographs with the object of comparing the styles and the alphabets.

1. Vallam.

Two miles to the east of Chingleput there stands a small hill where one arrives very easily by taking the high-road leading from Chingleput to Tirukkalukkunram. On the right side of the road stand the village and the hill of Vallam. There are three caves excavated on the east side of the latter. The largest of them contains inscriptions. We shall speak of the two others later on.

The Vallam inscriptions are mentioned in S. I. I. Vol. II, Part III, pages 340 and 341. The oldest of them is translated (No. 72) and reproduced (*Plate X.*)

This inscription is found on the two pillars at the entrance to the cave. The language and the alphabet are Tamil.

It says that the cave was cut by Skandasêna, son of Vasantapriyarâja and vassal of King Mahêndrapôtarâja who was surnamed Guṇabhara, Śatrumalla, Lalitâṅkura, Pagâppiḍugu. Here there is no doubt about the name of the king, since the word Mahêndra is followed by Pôta-Raja (*i.e.*) King of Pallavas.

However, we do not know if this Mahêndra is Mahêndravarman I, Mahêndravarman II, or a predecessor of Siṁhavishnu, who is mentioned in the Vâyalûr inscription (see *G. O.*, No. 538, 28th July 1909, page 77). It is, however, proper to add that this last king's existence is highly problematical, considering that much credit cannot be given to the list of the

25 kings mentioned in the Vâyalûr inscription as the predecessors of Siṁhavishṇu.

A fourth Pallava prince of the name of Mâhêndra was the son of Râjasiṁha (vide *S. S. I.* Vol. I, No. 27, pages 22 and 23.)

It is not however probable that this Mahêndra was the contemporary of Skandasêna who excavated the Vallam cave. The son of Râjasiṁha lived at the begining of the 8th century, and the form of the alphabet used in the Vallam inscription belongs to an earlier period.

Pl. IX, A, shows the plan of the Vallam cave. From *Pl. IX, B*, we can get an idea of the form of one of the pillars. On both sides of the façade are found bas-reliefs; on the right stands Jyêshthādēvī considered here undoubtedly as the wife of Śiva and on the left Gaṇeśha probably considered as the son of the same god. This image of god is represented in my *Archéologie du Sud de l'Inde*, (Vol. II, *Pl. XVI. B.*)

The sanctuary contains a liṅgam; there is every reason to believe that it is as old as the temple itself. It is remarkable that this liṅgam is cylindrical and not at all prismatic as those of the epoch of Râjasiṁha.

On each side of the entrance to the sanctuary stand two dvârapâlas, door-keepers of the temple.

Plate VIII shows the image of the dvârapâla on the left side. It was very difficult to photograph this bas-relief, as the interior of the temple is dark and narrow.

It is the front view; the legs are crossed. He has a terrible aspect. His head crowned with hair is adorned with horns.

The pose of the hand which rests on the club deserves special attention. We shall have occasion to find the

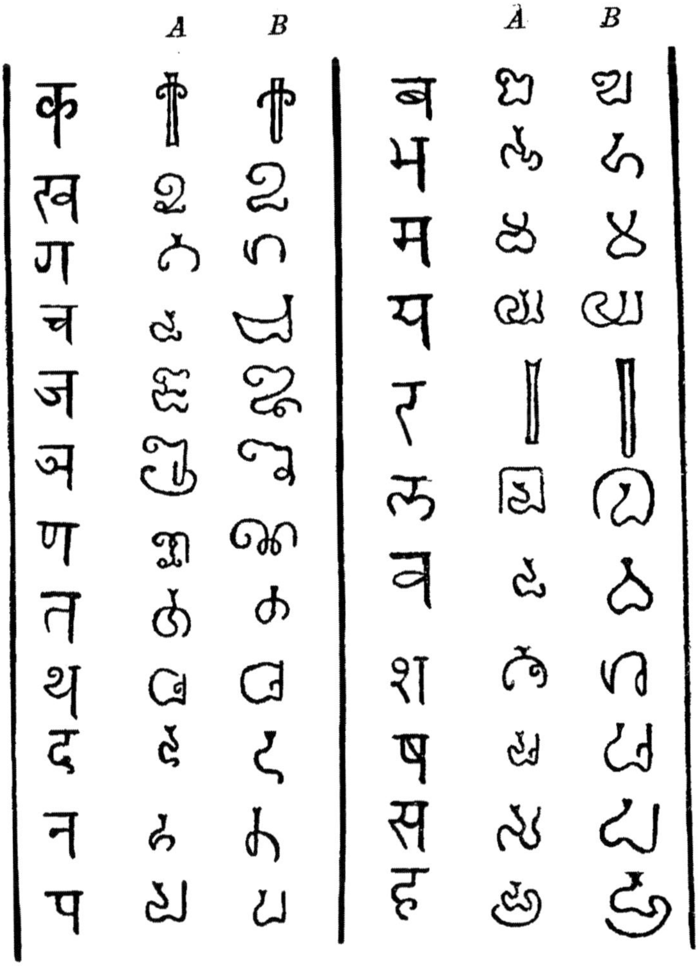

Comparison of the alphabets of Râjasimha.

A. Florid alphabet (Kaïlâsanâtha temple at Kâñchîpuram.)

B. Simple Alphabet (Panamalai.)

Plate VIII.

(VALLAM.)

Left dvârapâla at Vallam.

same special pose in other monuments of the same kind.

The dvârapâla on the right resembles the one on the left.

I shall here make a general remark about the monuments of the Pallava period: the Dvârapâlas have only two hands. It is only after this period that the sculptors gave them four hands, and this plurality of hands has become the rule from the end of the 8th century.

2. Mahêndravâdi.

This village is situated 3 miles to the south-east of the Sholinghur Railway Station near Arkonam (North Arcot District).

Not far from the village is a large tank which perhaps owes its origin to the Pallavas. The village is inhabited by Vaishnava Brahmans.

To the east extends a plain on which there stands a big rock. The rock-cut temple is on the eastern side of this rock. The inscription is written on the pilaster which is at the left end of the façade. The translation of it has been published in page 153 of Vol. IV of *Epigraphia Indica.*

The reproduction of this inscription by "estampage" is found in the plate facing page 152 of the same work; however, as the form of the letters cannot be easily distinguished in the estampage, we thought it would be useful to take on the spot a fac-simile of the inscription which will be found in *Pl. X.*

The inscription says that Guṇabhara dug the cave called Mahêndra - Vishṇugṛiha in the city of Mahêndra on the bank of the tank of Mahêndra.

From *Pl. XIII A*, one can get a clear idea of the very simple style of the façade.

The pillars (*Pl. XII, A.*) are like those at Vallam. They are square in section, the middle third of which has been made prismatic by chamfering off its corners.

The brackets that support the vault have a curved profile instead of the rectilinear one found at Vallam. The difference however is not very great.

The faces of the cubical parts are adorned with lotus flowers and varieties of rosework sculptured in very low relief. *Pl. XII, B*, shows the plan of the "cave". *Pl. XIII, B*, will give an idea of the dvârapalas; they present a full front view and have a calm pose as befits a temple of Vishṇu.

These sculptures have been obliterated by the mouldering of the stone.

The sanctuary contains a clumsy statue of Narasiṁha which is not at all antique.

3. Dalavânûr.

This village is situated in the Tindivanam Taluq (South Arcot District) 5 miles to the west of Perani Railway Station.

The cave is cut in the southern side of a small hill lying in the north of the village and called "Pañcha Pâṇḍava Malai".

It is here necessary to rectify an error regarding the position of the inscription. In the report on Epigraphy (*G. O.* No. 518, 18th July 1905) the inscription written in the Sanskrit language with Grantha-Pallava characters is found, under No. 51 of 1905, mentioned as follows: "on the same pillar" as the inscription No. 50, which is referred to as being "on one of the pillars inside the same cave." It would appear then that the inscription is on one of the two pillars which are inside the cave. When I visited Dalavânûr, I searched for it at the abovementioned spot but in vain. I found the inscription on the pilaster of the façade which is at the left end.

Though placed outside and exposed to rain, the inscription has been admirably preserved and it was easy for me to obtain a very neat 'estampage' of it which will be found in *Pl. XVI, A.*

The inscription has been reproduced and translated (vide *Ep. Ind.*, Part V, Vol. XII, January 1914, p. 225). It says that the cave was cut by King Narêndra surnamed Satrumalla. *Pl. XVI, B,* shows the plan of the cave.

An interesting peculiarity is that the shrine is not placed opposite to the entrance, but to the left of it. It is because the façade of the temple faces the south and the architect wished however that the shrine should face the east.

Pl. XVI, B, shows the entrance to the sanctuary and on each side is a Dvârapâla who raises his hand to his head in sign of adoration.

The sanctuary contains a liṅgam which is cylindrical as the one at Vallam and not prismatic as those of the epoch of Râjasiṁha.

The façade of the cave is ornamented at the ends with two Dvârapâlas representing the two types used at this epoch. The one on the left raises his hand as those placed at the entrance to the sanctuary : but the one on the right rests it on a club and the pose of the hand is similar to that of the Dvârapâla at Vallam shown in *Pl. VIII.*

The two pillars at the façade are of the same type

as those at Mahêndravâḍi *Pl. XII. A.* The cubical parts are ornamented with lotuses. The two pillars stand one on each side of the entrance to the cave, and above it there is an ornament which is shown in *Pl. XVI, A.* It is nothing but the 'tiruvatchi' we have already mentioned.

The 'tiruvatchi' at Dalavânûr is formed of two arches emerging from the mouth of fabulous animals; the two arches join in the middle, where there is a small platform supporting a Gandharva.

We shall call this form of decoration 'double-arched tiruvatchi,' to distinguish it from the 'single-arched tiruvatchi' of the epoch of Râjasiṁha.

The façade of the cave is surmounted by a cornice which is decorated with a Kûdu. The Kûdus at Dalavânûr are very well preserved and their design can therefore be seen very well. On the contrary, the other Pallava monuments have Kûdus the stone of which is much weather-beaten.

We see from *Pl. XVI, A*, that it is the Kûdu with the head of Gandharva surmounted by a "shovel-head" that characterises the Pallava art as it has been shown in '*Archéologie du Sud de l'Inde*,' Vol. I, page 96. In fact, after the Pallava period, the lion's head is used instead of the "shovel-head."

3. Sîyamangalam.

The name of this village being surely the same as Siṁhamaṅgalam, we can suppose that the original name was Siṁhavishṇu-chaturvēdimaṅgalam after the king Siṁhavishṇu, father of Mahêndravarman I.

The village is one mile to the south of Dêsûr (North Arcot District, Wandiwash Taluq).

The sanctuary of the temple is cut in a rock. There is a series of maṇḍapams before the shrine, so that, to arrive at the sculptured rock, one has to pass through many very dark halls, and it is only with the help of torch-light that one can see the part of the temple belonging to the days of the Pallavas.

I could not photograph anything here on account of the darkness that reigned in this place. I could only draw a few sketches.

The Sanskrit inscription written in Grantha-Pallava alphabet is engraved on one of the pillars of the façade. It is in such a dilapidated condition that some letters are almost invisible. The 'estampage' of it published in *Epigraphia Indica*, Vol. VI, No. 32, p. 320, does not enable us to distinguish the form of the letters.

We therefore thought it necessary to take a facsimile of it on the spot; it will be found in *Pl. XVII. A.*

The alphabet is similar to those of Dalavánûr (*Pl. XIV. A*) and Mahêndravâdi (*Pl. X*), but it completely resembles that of Dalavânûr.

In *Pl. XI*, we have compared the alphabet of Mahêndravâdi, Dalavânûr and Śîyamaṅgalam with that of Panamalai, only on account of some letters that differ most. The two alphabets are simple and not at all florid. The differences existing between them are, however, so numerous that we can affirm that the Dalavânûr and Sîyamangalam inscriptions are anterior to that of Panamalai by one century.

Lastly, it has to be noted that Dalavânûr, Sîyamaṅgalam and Panamalai are very near one another, all of them being situated in the Gingee hills. The difference in the alphabets cannot therefore be explained by a difference in the districts.

The inscription at Śîyamaṅgalam attests to the excavation of the temple of Avanibhâjana-Pallavêśvara by King Lalitâṅkura (*Ep. Ind.*, Vol. VI, p. 320, No. 32.)

Pl. XVII, B, shows that the plan of the cave is nearly the same as that of the one at Mahêndravâḍi.

The shrine contains a liṅgam which is cylindrical and not prismatic. On both sides of the entrance to the shrine are found dvârapâlas having this important peculiarity that they are almost like those at Vallam.

On both sides of the façade are placed certain personages whose special attitude is a unique point in the Pallava art. They are men having moustaches and brandishing sticks.

Pl. XVIII represents the man on the left. He is placed in a niche which we see is ornamented with a "double-arched Tiruvatchi" like that of Dalavânûr.

The two pilasters that are on either side of the niche supporting the decoration also deserve our attention. The table of the abacus is formed of two doucines.

This kind of abacus is very archaic and resembles the abacus of the monuments of the Buddhistic period (Amarâvatî) which has the form of a staircase turned upside down.

Pl. XIX represents a pillar of the façade of the cave.

It is a pillar square in section like those of Vallam, Mahêndravâḍi, and Dalavânûr. A lotus is carved on the lower cube and a lion is seen standing on the upper one. We may think that, if the cave belongs to the time of Siṁhavishṇu, this lion is the symbol of the king, who, in the Kaśâkûḍi plates, is called Avanisiṁha (the lion of the earth.)

The bracket has a circular profile as at Mahêndra-

Plate IX.

A. Map of the upper cave at Vallam.

B. Pillar in the same cave.

Plate X.

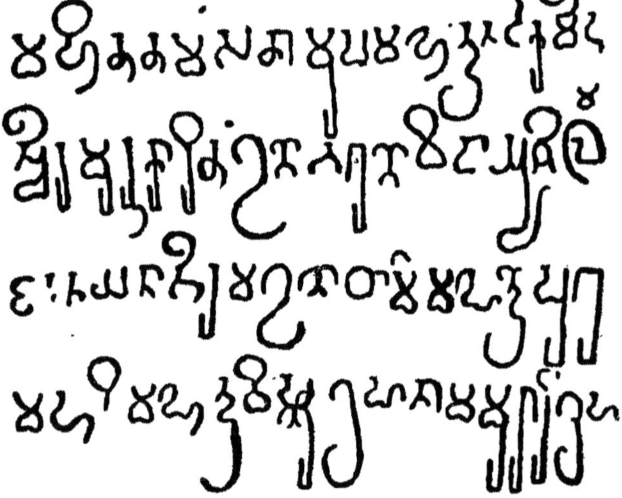

Pallava inscription at Mahêndravâdi.

vâḍi and Dalavânûr. However, it is adorned with scroll-work like those at Trichinopoly.

5. Pallâvaram.

M. R. Ry. H. Krishna Sastri writes (*G. O.*, No. 538, 28th July 1909, page 75): "The present station of Pallâvaram on the South Indian Railway is distinct from old Pallâveram, which is a ruined village about two miles south of the Railway station." The Pañcha Pâṇḍava Malai, the side of which has been excavated by the Pallavas, is not to the south of the station but to the east.

The cave, which is in the hands of the Muhammadans, is in a regrettable condition. One part of it is closed up with mud walls; and all the walls are covered with a thick coating of lime. Again, the inscription in Grantha-Pallava characters is inaccessible in those parts of the cave that are closed up, and in all other places it is covered with lime.

The inscription consists of a single line all along the entablature above the pillars. It is engraved over the whole length, not only of the façade, but also of the first inner lobby. It is made up of a series of names which are evidently the titles or "birudas" of a king (*Vide G. O.* No. 538, 28th July 1909, Page 75, Part II, No. 14). It is noteworthy that the first name in the series is Sri - Mahêndra - Vikrama. It is very probable that the King who cut the cave was called Mahêndra.

As we have already said, the form of the letters is not like that of those at Dalavânûr, Śîyamaṅgalam and Mahêndravâḍi.

The beginning of the inscription is reproduced as a specimen in *Pl. XXI, A.* We read: Śrî-Mahêndra-Vikramaḥ, Mattavilāsaḥ, Chetthakâri, Vichitrachittah. One peculiarity about this inscription is that most of the other names are incomprehensible and seem to be words of Telugu origin.

However, among the epithets are found the name Lalitâṅkura which exists in the Śîyamaṅgalam inscription, and Pugâpiḍuka (Pagâppiḍugu) which is found in the Vallam inscription.

Pl. XX shows the plan of the cave.

There are five shrines corresponding to the five gateways. Probably they were each occupied by a liṅgam and the temple was dedicated to Śiva.

The pillars are exactly of the same type as those at Mahêndravâḍi but without the lotus. It is however probable that the lotuses were painted on them.

6. Trichinopoly.

The "Upper cave" cut in the rock at Trichinopoly is covered with inscriptions.

On examining those of the inscriptions that are written in the Grantha-Pallava alphabet, I have ascertained the following facts:

1° The series of names of the king which are engraved on the pillars are all written in the same alphabet as the inscriptions Nos. 33 and 34 of *S. I. I.*, Vol. I, Pages 28, 29, 30.

2° This alphabet is very much like that of Pallâveram.

3° There are no inscriptions written in a more archaic alphabet.

Alphabets compared :

A. Alphabet of the inscriptions at Dalavânur, Mahèndravâdi, Siyamangalam.

B. Alphabet of the inscription at Panamalai.

Plate XII.

A. Pillar at Mahêndravâdi.

B. Map of the cave at Mahêndravâdi.

Most of the names written on the four pillars at the façade of the cave are reproduced in *Pl. XXIII.* The letters are excellently preserved and give a very correct idea of the alphabet employed. However, most of the names are incomprehensible and are perhaps of Telugu origin.

Mixed up with these, we find however the names: Nityavinîtaḥ, Nirapêksaḥ, Naihikâmutrikaḥ, Virasaḥ, Vyavasthitaḥ, Vyavasâyaḥ, Anumânaḥ, Avanibhâjanaḥ Akaruṇaḥ, Anityarâgaḥ.

Be it noted that we have already met with the name "Avanibhâjana" in the Śîyamaṅgalam inscription.

The pillars at the lower end of the cave contain also some names. The series begins on the left by the name Guṇabhara. We have said that the inscriptions Nos. 33 and 34 of *S. I. I.*, Vol. I., p. 28, contain the names Guṇabhara, Śatrumalla, Purushottama and Satyasaṁdha. All these details are found mentioned in the Annual Report of the Director-General of Archæology for 1903-04, p. 271.

I believe, however, that sufficient stress has not been laid on the following fact.

To the right of the shrine, on one of the pilasters of the façade and at a spot which seems to have been selected for the principal inscription, there are certain engravings in Grantha-Pallava characters.

The inscription begins solemnly with the word "Svasti", then follow the names, Srî Mahêndravikramaḥ, and Mattavilâsaḥ, exactly as in the Pallâvaram inscription.

Pl. XXIV, A represents a copy of what I consider to be the principal inscription at Trichinopoly.

There is no doubt :

1° that the king who excavated the shrine was called Mahêndra, since this name is found in the place of honour ;

2° that this king is no other than the one who excavated the Pallâvaram temple, since the Pallâvaram inscription begins likewise with the names Sri Mahêndra-vikrama and Mattavilâsa written in the same alphabet.

The plan of the Trichinopoly cave will be found in *Pl. XXIV, B.*

The pillars of the façade are like those of Vallam. The brackets however are of scroll-work as at Sîyamaṅgalam. The cubical parts are ornamented with lotus flowers as at Dalavânûr.

The façade of the Trichinopoly cave is shown in the 'Archéologie du Sud de l'Inde,' Vol. I., *Pl. XXII, A.*

On entering the shrine, we find, on the left, the bas-relief representing Śiva holding the Gaṅgā in his matted hair. This is shown in the same book Vol. I, *Pl. XXII, B* and Vol. II, *Pl. XI, B.*

The sanctuary of the temple is on the right of the entrance. It probably contained a liṅgam that has since been taken away.

From *Pl. XXII* we can form an idea of the dvârapâlas defending the entrance to the sanctuary.

We remark at once that their hands are placed on a club in the same manner as those of the dvârapâlas at Vallam (vide *Pl. VIII.*) and at Śíyamaṅgalam ; their legs are crossed in the same manner ; the general aspect is the same.

Plate XIII.

(MAHÊNDRAVÂDI.)

A. Facade of the cave at Mahêndravâdi.

B. Dvârapâlas at Mahêndravâdi.

Plate XIV.

(DALAVÂNÛR.)

A Inscription at Dalavânûr.

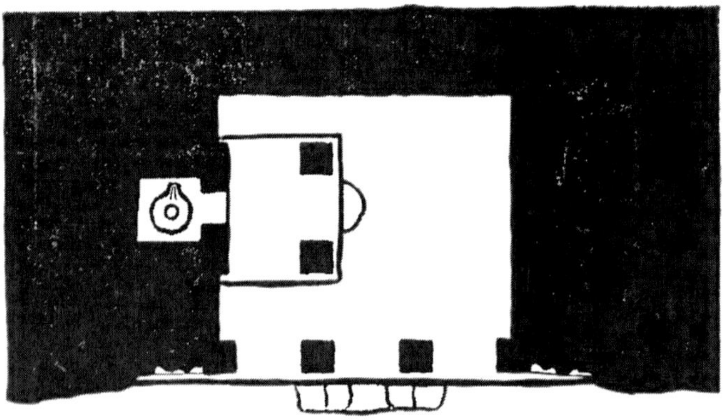

B. Map of the cave at Dalavânûr.

Conclusion.

The alphabet of the Trichinopoly and Pallâvaram inscriptions seems to be less archaic than that of Mahêndravâḍi, Dalavânûr and Śîyamaṅgalam. One may be inclined to think that the Mahêndra of Trichinopoly is not the same as he of Mahêndrâvaḍi, the one being, for instance, Mahêndravarman I, the other Mahêndravarman II.

However, the similarity of the names (birudas) of the king, and, above all, the great resemblance of the style of the sculptures induce us to form a contrary hypothesis.

We shall admit that at the same epoch there existed two Grantha-Pallava alphabets; the one, that of Mahêndravâḍi, Dalavânûr and Śîyamaṅgalam, very simple; and the other, that of Trichinopoly and Pallâvaram, more ornate, almost florid, in which the straight lines have a tendency to become curved and turned.

We shall admit that the caves of Vallam, Mahêndravâḍi, Dalavânûr, Śîyamaṅgalam, Pallâvaram and Trichinopoly belong to the same period, that of a king who bore the names of Guṇabhara (Trichinopoly, Vallam, Mahéndravâḍi), Lalitâṅkura (Trichinopoly, Vallam, Pallâvaram, Śîyamaṅgalam), Śatrumalla (Trichinopoly, Vallam, Dalavânûr), Mattavilâsa (Trichinopoly, Pallâvaram), Pagâppidugu (Vallam, Pallâvaram), but whose principal name, which is found at Trichinopoly, Pallâvaram, Mahêndravâḍi and Vallam, was Mahêndra, and that this Mahêndra is Mahêndravarman I.

We have many reasons to think so:

1° The alphabets of Mahêndra are less developed than that of Panamalai and make us believe that they differ in age by about one century.

2° The other princes named Mahêndra, and particularly Mahêndravarman II, seem either to have reigned for a very short time or not to have reigned at all.

However, the most conclusive reason seems to be the following: the second verse of inscription No. 33 (*S.I.I.*, Vol. I., p. 29) at Trichinopoly contains a passage, "King Guṇabhara......which has turned back from hostile conduct," which seems to be an allusion to the fact that King Guṇabhara, that is to say, Mahêndra, was once an enemy of the Sivite religion and was afterwards converted to the cult of the liṅgam.

If, then, we admit with V. Venkayya (*Ep. Ind.*, Vol. III, p. 277) that Mahêndravarman I. persecuted the saint Appar and was afterwards converted by him and that, on the other hand, Appar belonged to the generation which preceded that of King Narasiṁhavarman I, it seems to be highly probable that King Guṇabhara of Trichinopoly is the King Mahêndravarman I.

It may not be impossible that the Sîyamaṅgalam (Siṁha-maṅgalam) temple which contains images of the lion and the inscription of King Avanibhâjana, belongs to the days of King Siṁhavishṇu (called Avanisiṁha in the Kâśakūdi plates). It is not impossible, in fact, that the "birudas" such as Śatrumalla, Lalitaṅkura, Avanibhâjana were borne also by Mahêndra and by his father Siṁhavishṇu.

Be that as it may, the sculptures of the six caves that we have studied enable us to determine the style of the epoch of Mahêndra which presents the following characteristics ;

1° Lingams cylindrical and never prismatic.

2° Dvârapâlas, always front view, hand sometimes resting on a club with a very peculiar pose and sometimes raised to the head in sign of adoration.

3° Pillars, square in section, adorned with lotus flowers.

4° " Double-arched Tiruvatchis."

5° Finally, we notice that the monuments that could be attributed to the epoch of Mahêndravarman I. are all of them rock-cut temples.

CHAPTER III.

CLASSIFICATION OF THE ANTIQUITIES OF THE PALLAVA PERIOD.

Mahêndravarman I. reigned in the first years of the VII century, and Râjasiṁha in the first years of the eighth. The corresponding styles, separated by an interval of one century, will serve as land-marks to determine the age of Pallava monuments.

Let us first determine the boundary of the country where there are antiquities attributed to the Pallavas.

From a certain number of copper plates bearing inscriptions, we are led to think, that, about the IV, V and VI centuries, the Pallava empire extended not only over the region of Kâñchîpuram but also over all the district of Nellore up to the mouth of the Godavari and the Kishna.

However, from the point of view of the monuments and the stone inscriptions, the Pallava country is more limited.

We do not know any Pallava monuments situated to the north of the river Swarnamukhi: « The only Pallava stone inscription found in the Nellore District is built into the floor of the Subrahmaṇya temple at Mallam in the Gûdûr Taluk. It is dated in the 15th year of the reign of the Pallava King Nandippôttaraśar.» (*Ind. Ant.*, Vol., XXXVII, p. 352.)

Plate XV.

(DALAVÂNÛR.)

Facade of the cave-temple at Dalavânûr.

Plate XVI.

(DALAVÂNÛR.)

A. Sculptures at Dalavânûr.

B. Dvârapâlas near the sanctuary at Dalavânûr.

It is not probable, again, that any monument situated to the south of the Southern Vellaur (Pudukkōttai State) could be attributed to the Pallavas.

The southernmost Pallava monument is the cave of Kunnāndârkôyil (Pudukkōttai State), the inscriptions in which (Nos. 346, 347 and 348), belonging to the time of Kings Nandi and Danti (*G. O.*, No. 1260, August 25th 1915), indicate the last years of Pallava sovereignty.

The cave of Śiva at Nârttâmalai belongs probably to the time of the king Ganga-Pallava Nripatuṅga (*G. O.*, No. 518 of 1905 and No. 365 of 1904).

Lastly, the inscription at Kuḍumiyâmalai, which is so interesting from a musical point of view and belongs probably to the beginning of the VII century, is written in characters similar to those of Trichinopoly. But there is nothing to show that Kuḍumiyamalai was under the direct rule of Mahêndravarman I.

In the west, the inscriptions in the caves of Nâmakal seem to show that the Salem region was under the domination, not of the Pallavas, but of the Koṅgu kings.

In short, from the point of view of the monuments, we think that the Pallava kingdom extended all along the Coromandel coast from Kâḷahasti in the north to Puduḳōttai in the south and was bounded in the west by the Eastern Ghats.

In that part of South India that we have delimited, apart from the numerous prehistoric remains, we know no ancient ones older than those of the Pallavas.

An exception must however be made in the case of "the beds of the Pâṇḍavas" which are perhaps very old.

We know that in the districts of Madura and Tinnevelly the caverns containing the "Beds" often have Brâhmî inscriptions which probably are very ancient.

Unfortunately, caverns of this kind which have been found to the north of the Cauvery contain no inscriptions.

On my way to Sîyamangalam, I was informed of the existence of similar "Beds" at Kilangunam (North-Arcot district, Wandiwash Taluk), a village 5 miles to the south of Dêsûr.

At Mâmbalappattu railway station (South-Arcot district, Villupuram Taluk) I heard of the existence of "Beds" in the adjacent rocks.

Lastly, when going to Gingee, Singavaram and Mêlachêri, I questioned the villagers about the antiquities of that region. It is thus I discovered a cavern at Kâvakkâdu, a village on the Tindivanam-Gingee road, which is two miles to the east of Gingee.

This cavern must have been a small monastery as there are more than 15 beds carved in the stone.

The cavern of Armamalai.—

Certain caverns were fitted up to serve as places of Hindu worship. Such is the cavern of Armamalai which is to the west of the villages of Malayampattu and Kârapattu (North Arcot District, Gudiyâttam Taluk).

These are the circumstances under which I was led to discover this cave:

The Udayêndiram plates mention that the King Nandivarman-Pallavamalla made a gift of the village of Kumâramangalam. I thought that the village was perhaps the one called Komaramangalam which is midway between Vaniyambadi and Ambur railway stations.

I therefore went to the village and tried to find out its boundaries with the help of the information contained in the Udayêndiram plates.

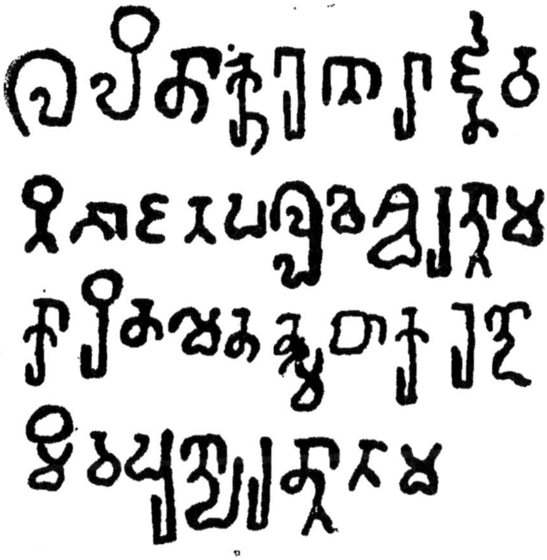

A. Pallava inscription at Siyamangalam.

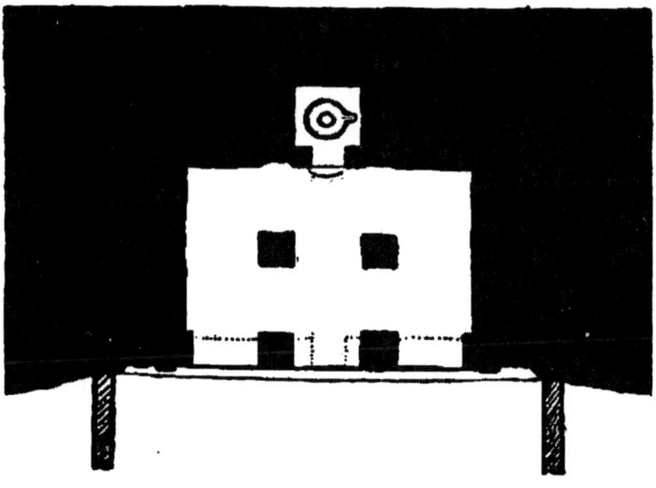

B. Map of the rock-cut temple at Siyamangalam.

Plate XVIII.

Sculptures at Siyamangalam.

They say (*S. I. I.*, Vol. II, Part III, p. 372) : « Its » western boundary (is the hill called) Lôhitagiri; » going north from this (the western boundary is) on the » east of (the hill called) Vêḷâlaśikhara; and on the » west of (the hill called) Kṛishṇaśilaśilôchchaya (the » cave called) Rauhiṇaguhâ.»

It is thus that I was led to visit the mountain which is situated between the villages of Malayampattu and Kârapattu and which, the natives told me, was called Armamalai.

Having arrived at the west slope of this mountain, I asked the people if there was not a cave near that place. They replied, that, in fact, there was a cavern and showed me the way to it in the midst of the rocks. It is a natural cave, sufficiently spacious, at the bottom of which there is a reservoir of water.

Unfortunately, there is not any ancient inscription in it.

It is certain that this cavern contained a shrine at the time of the Pallavas; for, we find there two stones on which dvârapâlas armed with clubs have been carved. Their costume, their ornaments and their form show, for certain, that these bas-reliefs belong to the Pallava period. The design, however, is very archaic and it is probable that these images are the oldest sculptures that could be attributed to the Pallavas.

As these dvârapâlas are adorned with serpents, it is highly probable that the shrine was dedicated to Śiva.

On the rock which overhangs and thus forms the roof of the cavern, we see numerous traces of paintings. Unfortunately it is impossible to find out what they represent, except in one place where we perfectly recognise the lotuses and the creepers.

These are the only paintings of the Pallava period that remain to us. I believed that the paintings in the Tirumalai (6 miles east of Polûr) cavern were old, but, when I saw them, I found out that they were all modern and not interesting.

The "cave" of Kîlmâvilangai—(South Arcot District, Tindivanam Taluk):—

It was by chance, that I discovered in 1915, a small rock-cut temple, which, from its archaic sculptures, appears to be the oldest shrine of this kind.

I took the road from Tiṇḍivanam to Dêsûr with the object of visiting Śîyamaṅgalam.

When passing through a small village which is at a distance of about a dozen miles from Tiṇḍivanam, I questioned the people in the hope of discovering a rock-cut temple. The villagers replied that they had never seen anything of the kind. One of them, however, who was questioned closely, declared that there was something of the kind at the very place we were in. In fact, a mere look in the direction pointed out by him was enough to perceive a small rock in which a shrine of Vishṇu, that was called the "Mukara-Perumal temple" had been hollowed out.

Pl. XXV, A, shows the general aspect of it. At the entrance stand two dvârapâlas holding a kind of flower in their hand. These personages are only sketched on the stone; the design is very primitive.

At the lower end of the sanctuary and carved in high relief, there is the god Vishṇu holding his emblems "Saṅkha" and "Chakra" without flames, which is a sign of archaism.

The Kîlmâvilaṅgai cave contains no inscriptions.

A pillar at Siyamangalam.

Plate XX.

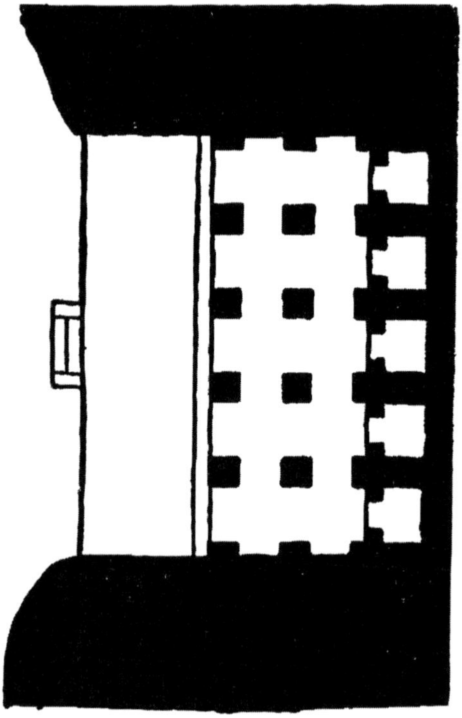

Map of the Pallava rock-cut temple at Pallāvaram.

Aragaṇḍanallûr (near Tirukoilûr, South Arcot District):—

Some of these rock-cut temples can be attributed to the Pallavas, though we cannot determine their exact age, as these "caves" do not contain any inscription or sculpture. This is the case, for example, of the "cave" of Aragaṇḍanallûr, the plan of which resembles in certain respects that of "the upper cave" at Trichinopoly, but which contains neither sculptures nor inscriptions. The stone is carved irregularly and artlessly.

Pañcha Pâṇḍava Malai (Kathivadi)—4 miles to the South-West of Arcot (North Arcot District):—

It is for the same reason that we cannot give the exact age of the rock-cut temple found in this place. Its plan resembles that of the Pallâvaram cave.

Singaperumâlkôyil—(Railway station near Chingleput):—

When I asked the villagers of Vallam and Pallâvaram about the rock-cut temples that might exist in that region, they mentioned to me the temple of Singaperumâlkôyil. So I went there and found one.

The shrine of god Narasiṁha, as well as the small veranda in front of it, is cut in the rock. When we get in by the entrance gôpuram we find ourselves in a large courtyard. Turning to the left we enter into a very dark building which is flanked in the south by a temple of "Agopala Valli" and in the north by the the temple of "Aṇḍal".

The main building consists of three chambers which must be crossed for reaching the portion cut in the rock.

The first chamber contains in the middle a statue of Hanumân and all along the northern wall a line of "Âlvârs."

The second chamber has only two dvârapâlas who stand at the entrance to the third one which contains a statue of Vishṇu placed in a recess in the north.

We are now in front of a small door through which we pass into the interior of the rock. Here we find a monolithic chamber which is in direct communication with the niche occupied by the god.

This part of the temple surely belongs to the Pallava period. However the inscriptions could not be distinguished at first sight owing to the darkness that is reigning there.

It was not possible for me to obtain from the priests permission to make a minute examination of this spot.

The Department of Epigraphy must direct their researches in that direction: they may find some inscriptions there.

I shall therefore confine myself to simply pointing out that the shrine in the Singaperumâlkôyil temple is cut in the rock and must be attributed to the Pallavas.

Kuraṇgaṅimuttam—(North Arcot District, Cheyyar Taluk):

It is probable that the cave situated in this place was attached to the village of Pallâvaram which still exists in the neighbourhood. We have not found in this cave any inscription of the Pallava period. It is true, that this temple, which is completely deserted by the villagers,—("This ancient monument is now deplorably neglected by the pious people of Kuraṅgaṇimuttam" *Vide G. O.*, No. 961, 2nd August 1913, p. 6.)—is also

Plate XXI.

(PALLÂVARAM.)

A B

A. Fragment of the inscription at Pallâvaram.

B. Facade of the cave-temple at Pallâvaram.

Plate XXII.

(TRICHINOPOLY.)

Dvárapálas near the sanctuary in the upper cave at Trichinopoly.

deplorably neglected by the Archæological Department. When I visited the cave in 1915, I observed that the earth which was covering it half way up hid many inscriptions of the age of the Chōḷas. It is not however probable that the clearing away of this earth would disclose any Pallava inscriptions.

This cave contains some sculptures representing Dvârapâlas. These are of a very archaic design. They present the front-view and are carved in very low relief. They somewhat resemble the dvârapâlas of the time of Mahêndra, but their attitude is less natural; they seem to belong to a previous epoch. I am led to believe that they belong rather to the end of the VI century than to the beginning of the VII.

Pl. XXV, B, will give an idea of the aspect of one of these dvârapâlas. The sculpture being damaged, it was impossible to make a drawing of it with greater precision.

Pl. XXV, C, shows the plan of this temple, which is distinguished from those of the other caves that we have so far studied, by the fact that at the end of every row of pillars there is a shrine.

These pillars are of the same type as those of Vallam.

Singavaram—(South Arcot District, Gingee Taluk):

In the "Madras District Gazetteers, South Arcot, by W. Francis, Vol. I., Madras, 1906, p. 366," the temple of Singavaram (2 miles north of Gingee) as well as the image of Vishṇu sleeping on the serpent are said to be cut out of the rock.

I therefore went to Singavaram with three objects in view:

1° To examine the style of the sanctuary to know if

its architecture would allow its being classed among the Pallava temples.

2° In that case, to find out if there were any inscriptions.

3° To examine if the image of the Sleeping God resembles the one at Mahābalipuram. This mission seemed difficult to fulfil, for the "Manual" says that Europeans are not allowed to enter the temple: "Europeans are not allowed anywhere near it."

Luckily, this order was not so strictly followed as I believed. After some pourparler, the priests allowed me to enter the first enclosure, then the second, and so on, till at last I found myself face to face with the deity.

It was in fact an Anantaśayana, and, as soon as I saw it, I recognised in it the work of the Pallavas. The right arm is stretched out and hangs down as at Mahābalipuram. The stone has however been sculptured newly at a later period.

The body of the Sleeping God is very large in size and extends from one end of the "cave" to the other. This cave consists of two verandahs with two pillars inside and two others at the façade. These pillars are similar to those of the Vallam "cave" but are decorated with lotus flowers.

At either end of the façade of the rock-cut temple there are two dvârapâlas that mostly resemble those found at the entrance to the shrine at Dalavânûr (*Pl. XVI, B.*)

There is therefore no doubt that the shrine at Singavaram belongs to the time of Mahêndra.

I shall here make a remark about the name of this place. It is very probable that Singavaram (that is to

Plate XXIII

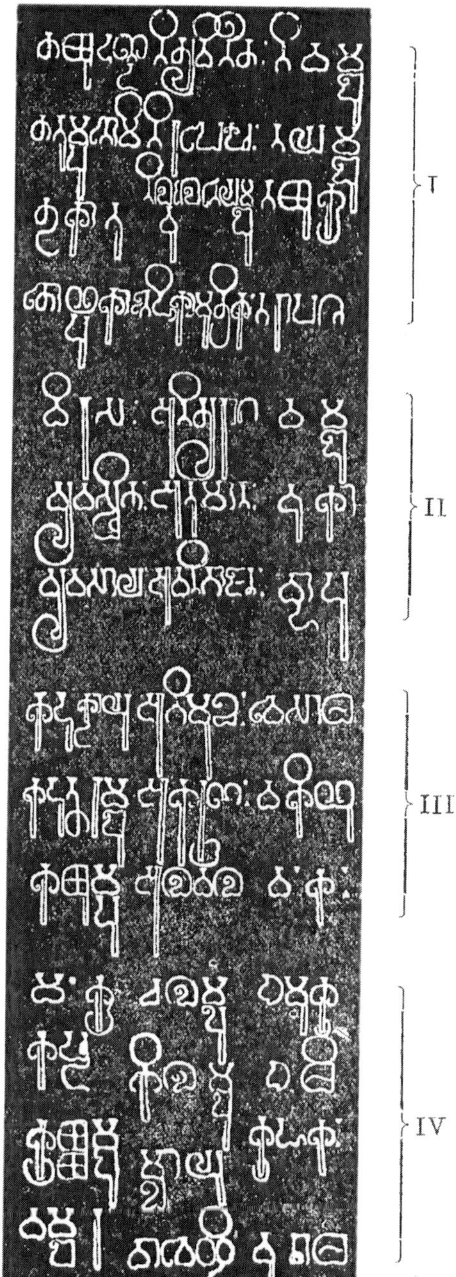

Inscriptions on the four pillars of the facade of the upper cave at Trichinopoly.

Plate XXIV.

A. Inscription of Srî-Mahêndra-Vikramah at Trichinopoly.

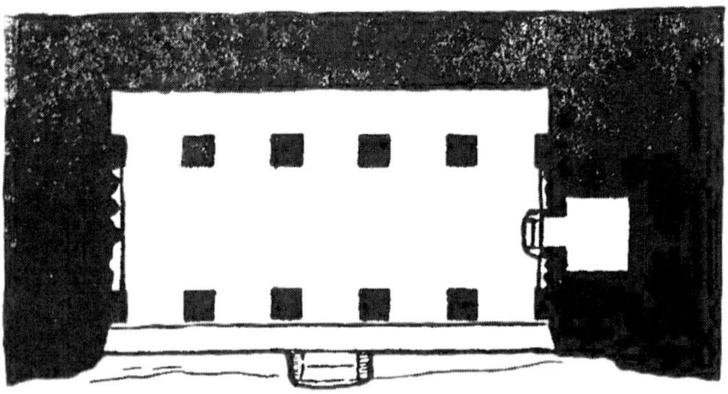

B. Map of the "upper-cave" at Trichinopoly.

say, Siṁha-puram) was the capital of Singapuranâḍu which contained the villages of Nerkuṇam (*G.O.*, 28th July 1909, No. 86 of 1908), Veḍâl (76 of 1908) and Tâyanûr (*G. O.*, 28th July 1910, No. 360 of 1909).

This name is therefore very ancient, and since the dvârapâlas of the Anantaśayana temple at Siṁha-pura are of the epoch of Mahêndra, we can safely suppose that Singavaram was founded by Siṁhavishṇu and that it is not impossible that the rock-cut temple was excavated during his time.

Luckily all hope of ascertaining the name of the king who cut this cave is not lost.

In fact, if I have not been able to find there any inscription of the Pallava period, it does not mean that it is impossible to find any.

If the Pallavas have put up any inscription in the temple, it must probably be on one of the pillars in the façade. But the surface of these pillars is hidden by the stones laid here to support the vault of the maṇḍapam that is built in front of the " cave."

If therefore the Department of Epigraphy could clear these pillars temporarily, they will probably discover there an inscription in Grantha-Pallava characters.

In his letter dated 10th March 1916, M. R. Ry. H. Krishna Sastri has been good enough to assure me that the temple of Ranganâtha which has been visited by the Government Epigraphist in 1903-4 will be again examined with the object of finding out if there exists any Pallava inscription on the pillars of the " cave."

It is desirable that this work should be done as early as possible.

Tirukkalukkunram—(Chingleput District and Taluk):

On the east side of the Vêdagirîśvara hill there is a rock in which the Orukal-maṇḍapam is excavated. (Vide *G. O.*, No. 538, 28th July 1909, p. 73).

The plan of this cave is similar to that of the shrine at Mahêndravâḍi (*Pl. XII, B*).

The pillars are of the same type as those at Vallam (*Pl. IX. B*).

The Liṅgam is cylindrical.

The Dvârapâlas are of the style of Mahêndra.

Pl. XXVI represents two of them. One of them (*Pl. XXVI, A*) stands at the right of the entrance to the shrine. It is big in size. The other (*Pl. XXVI, B*) has its hand raised to the head. It is elegant in form.

To the right of the sanctuary, there is a bas-relief representing Vishṇu, and to the left there is another representing Brahmā.

The latter image has a peculiar coiffure which is almost spherical and quite different from what is given to Brahmā in other Pallava sculptures (for example, Mahābalipuram).

These sure signs of great antiquity do not allow us to share the opinion of M. R. Ry. H. Krishna Sastri (*G. O.* No. 538, 28 July 1909, p. 76) who suggests that this cave must be contemporaneous with the "rathas" of Mahābalipuram.

We shall then conclude by saying "Orukal-maṇḍapam" belongs to the style of Mahêndra.

Dalavânûr, Śîyamaṅgalam, Mahêndravâḍi, Vallam, Pallâvaram, Trichinopoly:—

We have already studied these caves, which distinguish the age of Mahêndra, and which must be

Plate XXV.

A. Kilmavilangai— The cave-temple.

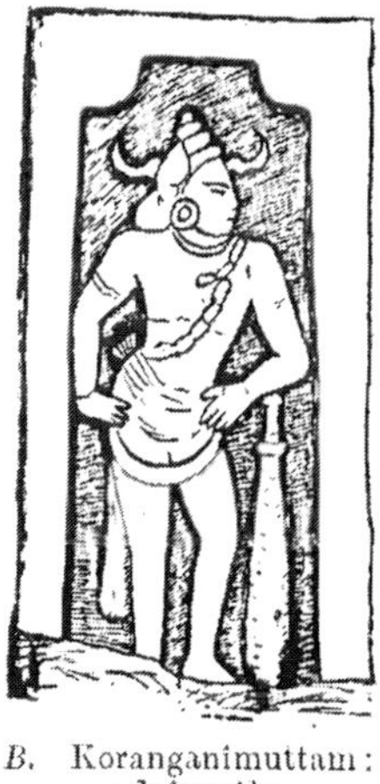

B. Koranganimuttam: a dvârapâla.

C. Map of the cave at Koranganîmuttam.

Plate XXVI. (TIRUKKALUKKUNRAM.)

A. Right dvârapâla near the sanctuary at Tirukkalukkunram.

B. Right Dvârapâla in a verandah in the cave at Tirukkalukkunram.

attributed to Mahèndravarman I., except those at Dalavânûr and Śîyamangalam which, as they do not contain the name of Mahêndra, could be attributed to Simhavishṇu.

Trichinopoly:—The lower cave resembles the upper one (Vide *Archéologie du Sud de l'Inde*, Vol. I, *Pl. XXI*) and that also could be attributed to Mahêndra.

Vallam—(Near Chingleput):—

We have said that there are three caves at Vallam and we have also described the upper one which contains the inscription of Mahêndra.

It is very probable that the two other "caves" date from the same epoch.

One of them dedicated to Śiva contains a cylindrical liṅgam and at the entrance to the sanctuary there stand two dvârapâlas resting their arms on a club in the style of Mahêndra.

The third cave, dedicated to Vishṇu, contains two dvârapâlas that raise their hands to their head and resemble the dvârapâla that stands in the left of the façade of the temple of Dalavânûr (*Pl. VII*).

Mâmandûr—(North Arcot District):

Six miles to the south of Kâñchîpuram, there is a stony hillock out of which four "caves" have been excavated.

The two caves in the north are attached to the village of Mâmandûr.

The two others that are more in the south are attached to a small village called Narasapoliem or Narasapuram.

Let us first take up the two "caves" in the north, i.e., the caves of Mâmandùr.

The right side cave contains a long inscription in Grantha-Pallava characters. A very large number of letters are visible; but, unfortunately, the stone is so damaged with vertical fissures that the lines of the inscription break off now and then and it is impossible to make any meaning out of it. Mr. E. Hultzsch who mentions this inscription (No. 38—*G. O.*, No. 424, 20th April 1888), declares that it is "illegible".

However, one important remark has to be made here: The alphabet is identically the same as that of Mahêndravâdi.

Pl. XXVII, B, is a photograph of a small part of the inscription which will enable us to judge of the form of the characters.

The cave was perhaps dedicated to Vishṇu.

The pillars of the façade, *Pl. XXVII A*, resemble much those of Mahêndravâdi. Particularly, the lotus flowers that adorn the cubical portions are exactly on the same model.

We may therefore conclude that from a palæographical and architectural point of view this "cave" belongs to the time of Mahêndravarman I.

The left side "cave" at Mâmandûr contains only Chôḷa inscriptions but its architecture and sculptures enable us to affirm that it very clearly belongs to the style of Mahêndra.

The pillars are of the Vallam and Tirukkalukkunram style. The central shrine contains a cylindrical liṅgam. The two others are empty.

The dvârapâlas are graceful and exactly of the style of Mahêndra.

Those that are at the entrance to the central shrine which is dedicated to Śiva have their arm on a club and resemble the dvârapâlas at Vallam, Śîyamaṅgalam and Trichinopoly.

The other dvârapâlas have their hands raised to the head in sign of adoration. The one in the extreme left at the end of the cave resembles much one of the dvârapàlas at Tirukkalukkunram (the one shown in *Pl. XXVI, B*).

The remnant of the paintings on the façade of the cave shows that the Pallava temples were painted.

In short, the two caves of Mâmandûr very clearly belong to the style of Mahêndra.

Narasapoliem—(near Mâmandûr):

The two caves that are found near this village to the south of the Mâmandûr caves and at a very short distance from them are left unfinished and without any inscriptions.

The right side one is very large and contains a series of shrines that probably contained liṅgams. There are no dvârapâlas.

The pilars are of the Pallâvaram type (*Pl. XXI, B*).

The left side cave, the southernmost one, is incomplete and uninteresting.

Tirakkôl—(near Dêsûr, North Arcot District, Wandiwash Taluk).

This village which is occupied by the Jaînas is a few miles to the north of Śîyamaṅgalam. When I visited the latter place I was informed that Tirakkôl contained a sculptured rock.

There is not precisely any " cave " in this place but only the outline of a temple hewed out of the rock. The two pillars at the façade are the only portions whose execution has been begun.

Maṇḍagappattu—(South Arcot District, Villupuram Taluk):

The inscription engraved on the façade, which is unfortunately in a very mutilated condition, leads us to believe that this cave at the back of which there are three niches was dedicated to the three gods Brahmā, Îśvara and Vishṇu. *Pl. XXIX, A*, is a fac-simile of the inscription in which the name of the king is not to be found (inscription No 56 of 1905, *vide G. O.*, No. 518, 18th July 1905, p. 47). We see that the alphabet is much like that of Dalavânûr, Śîyamaṅgalam, Mahêndravâdi.

The façade of the temple is interesting. *Pl. XXVIII* gives an idea of it. The dvârapâla on the right side that presents the front view and belongs to the style of Mahêndra, is noteworthy.

The dvârapâla on the left side (*Pl. XXIX, B*) is very much like those at the Trichinopoly cave.

The dvârapâlas being adorned with serpents, there is no doubt that, if the temple was dedicated to the Trinity, the principal God in it was Siva.

Rathas and "caves" of **Mahābalipuram** (the Seven Pagodas)—(Chingleput District and Taluk):

I have said in the "*Archéologie du Sud de l'Inde*" (Vol. I, Architecture p. 103) that the antique remains of Mahābalipuram are not all in the same style:

« When we were speaking of the Pallava monu-
» ments of the Seven Pagodas, we divided them into
» two groups:

« The first group comprising the rathas and caves,
» which are monolithic and the second comprising the
» temples that are not monolithic but built of stone.
» There are three of the latter kind : the first situated
» in the north of the village is unimportant ; the second
» is built near the light-house on the top of a rock in
» which the Durga cave is excavated, and the third
» which is at the sea side is known under the name of
» 'The Shore Temple.'

« A very attentive examination is not necessary to
» observe that the monuments of the second group are
» not in the same style as those of the first.»

Maintaining this division of the Pallava monuments of Mahābalipuram into two groups, 1° The Rathas and the caves cut in the rock, 2° The monuments built of stone (Shore Temple type), we shall first take up only the sculptured rocks, Rathas and caves that form the first group, and study them from two points of view : 1° the point of view purely architectural, 2° the point of view of inscriptions.

§ I. *The style of the Caves and Rathas of Mahābalipuram.*

From an examination of the style of the sculptures we are led to enunciate the following two propositions :

1° The Caves and Rathas of Mahābalipuram present certain marks of archaism that enable us to affirm that these monuments belong to an epoch anterior to that of Râjasiṁha.

(*a*) Nowhere, indeed, do we find the "Single-arched tiruvatchi" which was the only one used at the time of Rājasiṁha. On the contrary, the "Double-arched tiruvatchi" of the epoch of Mahêndra is found in many places: on each of the four faces of the "Draupadi-ratha", on the façade of the "Trimurti cave," in many parts of the "Rathas" found north-west of the bungalow on the bank of the Buckingham canal.

(b) Nor do we see anywhere on the caves and rathas the rearing lions of Râjasiṁha; the lions on them are always in a squatting and never in a rearing posture.

(c) Another proof is taken from Iconography. In our work ("Archéologie du Sud de l'Inde," Vol. II. Iconographie) we have stated many a time (pages 6–7 and pages 63–64) that the insignia of Vishṇu called "Śaṅkha" and "Chakra" have gone through a great evolution during the course of centuries and can therefore serve in ascertaining the age of the sculptures.

In the temple of Kailâsanâtha at Kañchîpuram, the sculptures are all coated with lime and it is almost impossible to know the exact form of the "Śaṅkha" and "Chakra" of the time of Râjasiṁha.

Luckily, I have been able to ascertain this point during my visit to Panamalai.

We have said that in the cleft of the rock containing the inscription of Râjasiṁha, translated and published in *S. I. I.* Vol. I, p. 24, there is an image of Mahishāsuramarddani (Kâli). This goddess always bears the Śankha and Chakra; and in the bas-relief at Panamalai, these insignia are in a very good state of preservation and we can observe their form very correctly. Well, then, we remark this peculiarity about them, that they are ornamented with *flames of fire.*

In the monuments of the epoch of Mahêndra, these weapons of Vishṇu are shown without the flames. Besides, in the rathas and caves of Mahâbalipuram these insignia of Vishṇu are represented without the flames.

It being admitted that the sculptors of the epoch of Râjasiṁha ornamented these weapons with flames of fire, we can conclude therefrom that the caves and rathas of Mahâbalipuram are anterior to the time of Râjasiṁha.

2° There is a certain resemblance between the caves and rathas of Mahabâlipuram and the monuments of the epoch of Râjasiṁha that enables us to affirm that the sculptured rocks of the Seven Pagodas belong to an epoch posterior to that of Mahêndra:

(*a*) We do not find anywhere in the monuments of the epoch of Mahêndra squatting lions at the base of the pillars. On the contrary, in the Kailâsanâtha temple at Kâñchîpuram there are numerous squatting lions. We shall therefore conclude that the squatting lion indicates an age posterior to that of Mahêndra.

The presence of numerous squatting lions in the caves and rathas of Mahābalipuram makes us believe that these monuments are posterior to the time of Mahêndravarman I.

(*b*) *Pl. XXX* represents one of the pillars of Mahābalipuram the like of which is very often met with in this place.

We remark not only the squatting lion but also the bulbous capital surmounted by a large abacus (palagaye), and nowhere in the art of Mahêndra do we see a pillar having such an abacus. This kind of pillars is, on the contrary, very numerous at Kâñchîpuram.

(*c*) We have given a long description of the dvârapâlas of the epoch of Mahêndra. We do not find the like of them anywhere at Mahābalipuram.

The dvârapâlas of the Seven Pagodas do not present the front-view but only the side-view and turn straight towards the shrine. (Note specially the dvârapâlas at the façade of the Trimurti cave. (*Pl. XXXI, A*). Nor do they rest their hands on a club as those found in the temples of Mahêndra. It must also be admitted that the dvârapâlas of the Seven Pagodas do not resemble those of Kâñchîpuram ; but they are in the style of an intervening period.

(*d*) We have said that in no place was the image of Sōmaskanda seen at the back of a shrine of the period of Mahêndra.

This image is seen at the sanctuary of Dharmarâja ratha at Mahabalipuram, but the execution is of a different type from that of Kâñchipuram.

(*e*) Nowhere in Mahabalipuram do we find the ornament of lotus flowers which is so often seen in the caves of Mahêndra.

In short, by their architectural style, the rathas and caves of Mahābalipuram appear to be more ancient than the monuments of Râjasiṁha but more modern than the temples of Mahēndravarman I.

The genealogy of the princes of tho dynasty of Siṁhavishṇu is well known. We know that only three kings have reigned between Mahêndravarman I. and Râjasiṁha ; they are :

Narasiṁhavarman I (about 625-650),
Mahêndravarman II (about 650),
Paramêśvaravarman I (about 655-690).

It is highly probable that the reign of Mahêndravarman II was very short.

We shall therefore conclude thus: By their style, the sculptures of the rathas and caves of Mahābali-

(MÂMANDÛR.)

A

B

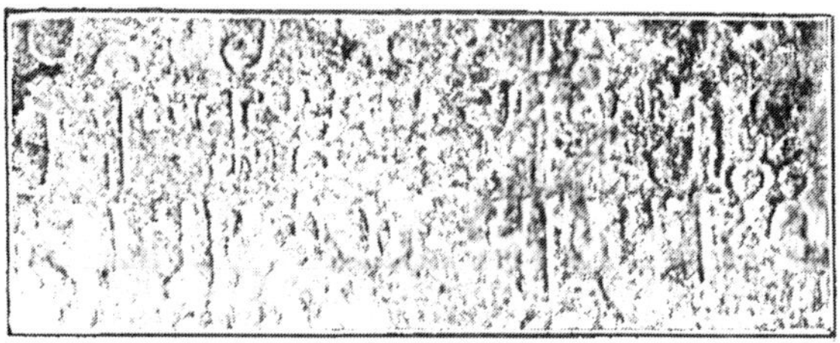

A Facade of the right cave at Mâmandûr.

B. Fragment of the inscription in the same cave-temple.

Plate XXVIII.

(MANDAGAPATTU.)

The Pallava rock-cut temple at Mandagapattu.

puram belong to the period of transition between the ages of Mahêndravarman I. and Râjasiṁha. It is therefore very probable that the rocks of the Seven Pagodas were carved during the reign of the two princes Narasiṁhavarman I. and Paraméśvaravarman I.

§ *II. The Inscriptions.*

The inscriptions engraved on the caves and rathas of Mahabalipuram can be divided into three groups, which we shall study successively :

(*a*) The first group of inscriptions is in an alphabet which greatly resembles those of the caves of Dalavâ-nûr, Śîyamaṅgalam, Mahêndravâḍi. Some of the letters and particularly the letter श, śa, are however less archaic. These inscriptions can therefore be attributed to the successor of Mahêndravarman I.

These inscriptions are found engraved on the Dharmarâja Ratha (*Vide S. I. I.*, Vol. I, Nos. 1 to 16, pp. 2 and 3). They are the "birudas" among which the name Srî-Narasiṁha occurs twice. None of these names are found in the inscriptions of Mahêndra. On the contrary, many of them, as Atyantakâma, Srîbhara, Sarvatobhadra etc., are among the "birudas" of Râjasiṁha.

The tenor of these inscriptions seems then to point also to a successor of Mahêndravarman I.

We may therefore conclude, that, according to

1° the form of the letters of the alphabet,

2° the tenor of the inscriptions,

3° the style of architecture,

the King that had the Dharmarâjaratha carved out is Narasiṁhavarman I.

Besides, the Trimurti cave contains three niches. That on the left, the northernmost one, contains an image of Subrahmanya (vide *Archéologie du Sud de l'Inde*, Vol. I, p. 84 and Vol. II, p. 49 and *Pl. XVIII, A*). And on the last step leading into this niche, I have found an inscription (*Pl. XXXI, C*) containing only two letters: मल्ल Malla, in characters similar to those of the inscriptions of Naraśiṁhavarman I. As we know that this prince had the cognomen of Mâmalla,[1] there is reason to believe that the inscription in the Trimurti cave must be attributed to this king.

Again, there is no doubt that the ancient name of Mahâbalipuram was Mâmallapuram. Therefore it is almost certain that Mâmallapuram was founded by Mâmalla or Malla, that is to say, by Narasiṁhavarman I.

(*b*) The second group of inscriptions are in the same florid style of the alphabet that we find in the Kailāsanâtha temple at Kâñchîpuram. They are the inscriptions in the Gaṇésa temple (*S. I. I.*, Vol. I, No. 18), in the Dharmarâja Maṇḍapam (*S. I. I.*, Vol. I, No. 19), in the Râmânuja Maṇḍapam (*S. I. I.*, Vol. I, No. 20) and in the third story of Dharmarâja Ratha (*S. I. I.*, Vol. I, No. 17).

The first two inscriptions are identical and are in praise of a king called Paramêśvara (vide *Ep. Ind.*, Vol. X, No. 1). From what we have said above, there is no doubt that this king is Paramêśvaraṿarman I.

1. *Indian Antiquary*, vol. IX, p. 100, and Plate; Bâdâmi fragmentary rock inscription of the time of the Pallava [Narasim]havishnu, named Mahâmalla, in the same alphabet that we find in the Dharmarāja Ratha at Māmallapuram (Mahâbalipuram).

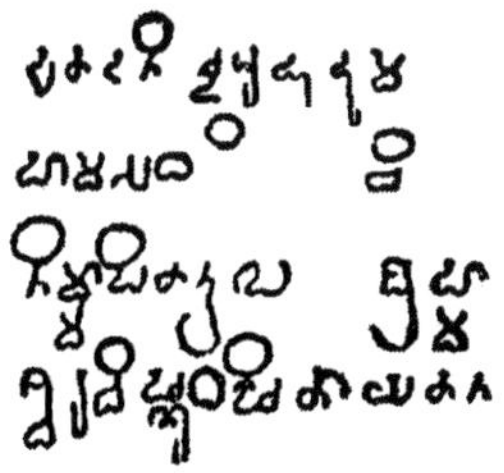

A. Inscription at Mandagappattu.

B. The left dvârapâla at Mandagappattu.

Plate XXX.

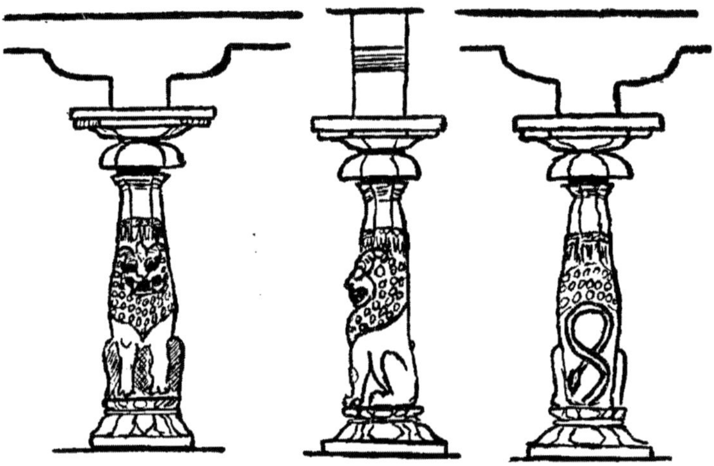

A pillar with a simha-basis at Mavaliveram.

This, however, only confirms the hypothesis that we put forward at the end of chapter II, that the florid alphabet of Râjasiṁha was created by his predecessor and that Râjasiṁha borrowed an alphabet that, at his time, was already archaic.

The inscription on the east side of the third story of Dharmarâja ratha (*S. I. I.*, Vol. I, No. 17) seems to show that the temple sculptured by Narasiṁhavarman I. was not consecrated by him but by his successor Paramêśvaravarman I., surnamed Atyantakâma, who gave it the name of Atyantakâma-Pallavêśvara.

(*c*) The inscription we have just spoken about, which is in florid characters, is written on the east side of the third story of Dharmarâja ratha. The same inscription is found also on the west side but in a non-florid form. The letters have not been cut deep enough and so the inscription remained unpreceived for a long time. It was discovered by V. Venkayya. This inscription is placed just above the entrance to the sanctuary, and like the one we have just mentioned, gives to the temple the name of Atyantakâma-Pallavêśvara.

The inscription is so short that it is not possible to determine exactly the kind of the alphabet it is written in.

However, holding an opinion contrary to that of M. E. Hultzsch (*Ep. Ind.* Vol. X, No. 1) I think that the two inscriptions on the third story of Dharmarâja ratha are contemporaneous and both are of the time of Paramêśvaravarman I. The only difference between the two inscriptions is that the one on the west side is in simple characters and that on the east is in florid characters.

We shall therefore conclude by saying that the tenor of the inscriptions, the form of the letters and the style of the sculptures are fully in accord to show that the caves and rathas of Mahâbalipuram were cut in the rock during the reign of Narasiṁhavarman I. (625 to 650) and that they were finished and consecrated during the reign of Paramêśvaravarman I. (about 675).

The large sculptured rocks, "Kṛishṇa uplifting the Govardhana mountain" and "Arjuna's penance" belong certainly to the same epoch, i.e., the middle of the seventh century.

Concerning the latter bas-relief, it is well to recollect that we cannot any more call it "Arjuna's penance." The merit of having given a satisfactory explanation of this scene goes to Mr. Victor Goloubew who has proved (*Asiatic Journal*, 11th series, Vol. IV, July-August 1914):

1° that the principal object in the scene is the vertical crevice in the rock, for, it is towards it that all the personages are turned;

2° that the presence of nâgas in this crevice proves the presence of water.

In that case all is clear. During the Pallava epoch the rain-water flowed through the crevice. This cascade then represented the Ganges descending to the earth from the heights of Kailāsa.

On the rock Śiva is seen giving an ear to the prayers of Bhāgîratha.

Thus the personage who has so long been mistakēn for Arjuna, is no other than Bhāgîratha, and this grand sight must be called not "Arjuna's penance", but "Bhāgîratha's penance".

(MAHABALIPURAM.)

A. Facade of the "Trimurti cave" at Mahabalipuram.

B. श्रीकधीति Sri-Kadhîti

Inscription discovered on the gopi-churn at Mahabali-puram.

B

C. मल्ल Malla.

Inscription on the floor of the left sanctuary of the "Trimurti cave" at Mahabalipuram.

C

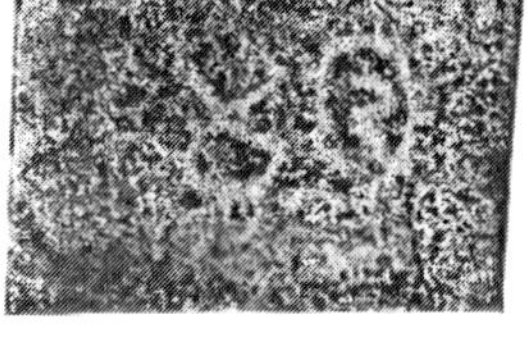

Plate XXXII.

(MÊLACHÊRI.)

Pallava inscription at Mélachéri.

Cave and inscription of **Mêlachêri** (near Gingee, South Arcot District):

In the *Madras District Gazetteer*, South Arcot, by W. Francis, Vol. I, page 364, we read: " Mêlachêri; three miles north-west of Gingee;...........The shrine of the temple to Maddileśvara to the north of the village and the liṅgam in it, are cut out of the solid rock of a low hill there."

I wished to find out:

1° if the temple cut out of the rock could be attributed to the Pallavas;

2° if there was any inscription in that temple. So I went to that place on the 1st January 1916 and ascertained that the shrine at Mêlachêri was a cave in the Pallava style and that one of the pillars of this rock-cut temple bore an inscription in Grantha-Pallava characters. This inscription was then unknown. M. R. Ry. H. Krishna Sastri, to whom I communicated the result of my investigations, was good enough to say in reply: " The inscription has not been copied by the Department and the credit of the discovery is all due to you."

Pl. XXXII is a reproduction of the "estampage" of the inscription at Mêlachêri.

M. R. Ry. S. Krishnaswami Aiyangar, Professor in the University of Madras, has been kind enough to translate it for me and it is given below:

Text.

Kāritam idam nṛpatinā
C(andrā) dity(ē)na s(ār)va(bhaumē)na
Śrī śikhari Pallavēśvaramiti
(Śai)vaṅ(dhā)ma siddh(ir) astu(gṛ.

Translation.

This Śiva temple named Śrī Śikhari Pallavēśvaram was built by King Chandrāditya, the Emperor. May Success attend.

The Alphabet used in this inscription resembles that of Narasiṁhavarman I. at Mahâbalipuram. It seems however to be somewhat less ancient.

It is therefore probable that the temple at Mêlachêri belongs to the middle of the VII century (about 650) and that Chandrâditya was one of the names of either Narasiṁhavarman I. or Paramêśvaravarman I.

The temple of Mêlachêri consists of a single verandah with two pillars at the façade and a shrine containing a cylindrical liṅgam.

There is not any bas-relief or decoration.

Sâḷuvaṅkuppam—(2 miles north of Mahâbalipuram):

The age of the antiquities of Sâḷuvaṅkuppam is a problem that has not been solved up to the present.

We know that the cave of Atiraṇachaṇḍêśvara in this place contains two inscriptions identical in tenor but written in two different alphabets.

The inscription on the northern wall (*S. I. I.*, Vol. I, No. 22) is written in Nâgarî-Pallava characters as that of the 1st and 4th lines at Kañchîpuram.

The inscription on the southern wall (No. 21) is written in Grantha-Pallava characters, as that of Panamalai and the second line at Kâñchīpuram. Writing about this subject Mr. E. Hultzsch says (*Ep. Ind.*, Vol. X, No. I, p. 3):

« As I have remarked in *S. I. I.*, Vol. I, p. 10, we » meet with the same plurality of the alphabets in the » Kailâsanâtha temple at Kâñchî. The enclosure of

» this temple bears three tiers of identical inscriptions.

« I am fully aware that my remarks on the third » and fourth alphabets do not rest quite on firm ground. » But in the absence of further information, we may » place the inscriptions written in both alphabets in » the time immediately preceding the conquest of the » territory by Vikramaditya (A. D. 733-734 to 746-747).»

After what we have said about the Panamalai inscription and the alphabets of Râjasiṁha, we cannot agree with Mr. E. Hultzsch who identifies Atiraṇachaṇḍa with Nandivarman-Pallavamalla.

In our opinion, the Sâḷuvankuppam cave belongs by its inscriptions to the time of Râjasiṁha.

And we find that an examination of the sculptures of Sâluvaṅkuppam also confirms this hypothesis :

1° The cave of Atiraṇachaṇḍa contains two prismatic liṅgams which characterise the epoch of Râjasiṁha.

2° Behind the liṅgams, at the back of the shrine, there are some images of Sōmaskanda resembling those at Kâñchîpuram.

3° The dvârapâlas at the entrance to the shrine have a very characteristic pose which is very much like that of the dvârapâlas in the Kailâsanâtha temple at Kâñchîpuram.

4° The "cave of lions" which is close by contains the rearing lions of Râjasiṁha.

It is therefore probable that Atiraṇachaṇḍa is none other than Râjasiṁha.

Besides, the name Atiraṇachaṇḍa figures in the inscriptions at Kâñchi (*S. I. I.*, Vol. I, No. 25, A. 3rd niche, p. 15) as well as in the inscription of Râjasiṁha at Tiruppôrur (*G. O.* No. 538, 28th July 1909, p. 77).

Certain reasons, however, lead us to believe that the Cave of Atiraṇachaṇḍa at Sâḷuvaṅkuppam is more ancient than the temples of Panamalai and Kâñchîpuram and that it must be ascribed to the beginning of the reign of Râjasiṁha, *i. e.*, the end of the seventh century (about 690 to 699).

Panamalai—(*vide* chapter I).

Temple of Kailâsanâtha at Kâñchîpuram — (*vide* Chapter I).

Mahâbalipuram—(The Seven Pagodas):

The small temple, which is near the light-house and on the summit of the rock out of which the "Yâmapuri maṇḍapam" has been carved, does not contain any inscriptions; but by its rearing lions, its dvârapâlas, its bas-reliefs, it belongs positively to the epoch of Râjasiṁha.

The same may be said of the small temple situated in the sands to the north of Mahâbalipuram and called "Mukundanayar Temple." It has no rearing lions, but its architecture, its liṅgam and the image of Sōmaskanda point to the time of Râjasiṁha.

The "Shore Temple" is quite in the style of Râjasiṁha. It bears no inscription of this king. However, it will be easily admitted that the "bali-pîtha" which is placed in front of the temple was built at the same time. As this contains some inscriptions of Râjasiṁha (*G. O.*, No. 961, 2nd August 1913, p. 89), it must be admitted that this king was the author of the "Shore Temple."

Tirukkalukkunram.—(Chingleput District and Taluk):

Near the summit of the Vêdagîri mount, by the

side of the way leading to the temple of Vêdagirîśvaıa, I found a pillar ornamented with a rearing lion of Râjasiṁha. This isolated piece of sculpture seems to have belonged to a temple which was probably built at the top of the rock at the time of Narasiṁha-varman II.

Tellâr—(North Arcot District, Wandiwash Taluq):

This village is 5 miles south-east of Dêsûr on the Tindivanam-Wandiwash road (vide *Madras Districts Manual, North Arcot,* Vol. II, Madras, 1894, page 445).

When travelling through this region I remarked here numerous remains of the Pallava period.

The shrine of the small temple in the north of the village is built of a large number of ancient stones.

By the side of the road, I found a bracket which surely belongs to the time of Râjasiṁha.

It is also certain that at Tellâr there was a temple in the style of Râjasiṁha.

Since Tellar existed during the Pallava period, it would not be impossible that it was at this place that King Ganga-Pallava Nandippôttaraiyar gained the victory of Tellaru, which won for him the title of Teḷḷârrerinda (vide, *e.g.*, *inscription* No. 180 of 1907).

Kâñchîpuram—(Conjeeveram):

It is probable that the temple of Vaikuṇtha-Perumal which was called Paramêśvara-Viṇṇagaram and which belongs to the style of Râjasiṁha was built by Paramêśvaravarman II. and finished by Nandivarman-Pallavamalla (*G. O.*, No. 492, 2nd July 1906, Part II, 2, page 61).

I shall however make a remark regarding certain sculptures. We know that the Vimâna of this temple is surrounded by a verandah which is covered with a long series of bas-reliefs of which only a very small number could be interpreted with the help of inscriptions explaining them. (Vide *G. O.*, No. 492, 2nd July 1906, p. 61). V. Venkayya, writing on this subject, says: « The four walls of the raised verandah which » runs round the central shrine of this temple, are » covered with two rows of sculptures separated by » a small belt, which was apparently intended for » engraving notes explaining the sculptures. They are » divided into a number of compartments each of which » was evidently meant to denote a particular event in » contemporary study.» I think that the idea that these sculptures refer only to contemporary events of the time of Nandivarman is not quite correct. These sculptures have a more general signification.

They represent the whole history of the Pallavas in pictures.

To understand these sculptures we must examine them beginning from the entrance gate and going all round the temple from left to right. The first panel (vide *Pallava Architecture* by *A. Rea, Pl. LXXXVIII*) represents Vishṇu, the second Brahma, and then successively Aṅgiras, Bṛihaspati, Samyu, Bharadvâja, Drôṇa, Aśvathaman. Here (vide *Pallava Architecture Pl. LXXXVIII*) a bas-relief represents the birth of Pallava and the litter of sprouts is cut by the side of a person who has his hands raised above his head and stands on one leg in the attitude of a penitent. This evidently illustrates verse 17 of the Kasâkûdi plates (*S. I. I.*, Vol. II, Part III, p. 355). [1]

1. " The glorious Pallava, (during whose rule) the earth was untouched " (even) by the smallest calamity, was suddenly born to him on a litter of

The rest of the series of bas-reliefs surely represent the continuation of the history of the Pallavas. Unfortunately the want of explanatory notes is an obstacle to the identification of these personages.

The temple of Muktêśvara at Kâñchîpuram, which contains an inscription of Nandivarman (No. 14 of 1893, *G. O.*, No. 642, 643 of 14th August 1893), belongs very probably to the time of Nandivarman-Pallavamalla.

The temples of Tirupurântakêśvara, Airâvatêśvara and Matañgêśvara, which belong to the style of Râjasiṁha (vide *Pallava Architecture*, by Alexander Rea, Madras, 1909), can be ascribed to the end of the VIII century.

It must be specially mentioned that the temple of Mataṉgêśvara contains dvârapâlas having four hands (vide *A. Rea*: *Pallava Architecture, Pl. XLV*). We have already said that the dvârapâlas of the Pallava period have only two hands. This exception seems to prove that the temple of Mataṅgêśvara belongs to the end of the Pallava period.

Kûram and Tiruppadikunram (near Kâñchîpuram):

The temples in these two villages, which are built in the Pallava style, also belong probably to the end of the Pallava period.

Tiruppattûr (Musiri Taluq, Trichinopoly District):

The temple of Kailâsanâtha at Tiruppattur does not contain any Pallava inscription. V. Venkayya (*G. O.*, No. 574, 17th July 1908) has admitted, however, that it is in the Pallava style.

" sprouts (Pallava) by (the nymph) Mênakâ, that had been sent to him by
" Sakra (Indra), who was afraid of (losing) his position (on account of the
" sage's austerities)."

According to the photographs No. 89 and 90 of 1907-08 that M.R.Ry. Krishna Sastri has kindly sent me, I think that this temple must be ascribed to the time of the Pallavas.

Tiruvadi (South Arcot District, Cuddalore Taluk):

When I visited the Siva temple at Tiruvadi, I remarked that the Vimâna of this temple strangely resembled that of Kailâsanâtha at Kâñchîpuram.

The plans of the two temples are alike: the Vimāna at Tiruvadi is surrounded by collateral niches.

The rearing lions are found in profusion.

Again, a priest affirmed that the shrine contained a prismatic liṅgam and an image of Sômaskanda. We know that the temple of Vîrattânêśvara at Tiruvadi contains (*G.O.*, Nos. 655 and 656, 24th July 1903) a few Pallava and Ganga-Pallava inscriptions (Nos. 56 and 36 of 1903).

It might not be impossible that the Vimâna was built at the end of the Pallava period and repaired later on, certainly at the time of the Chôḷas.

Tiruveḷḷarai—(Trichinopoly District):

I have visited the two rock-cut caves at Tiruveḷḷarai. They are very simple in architecture, and one of them situated in the enclosure of the Vishṇu Temple seems to have remained unfinished. They can be attributed to the kings belonging to the dynasty of Nandivarman (vide *G.O.*, No. 492, 2nd July 1906, p. 62) as bearing inscriptions connected with it.

So they are probably contemporaneous with the Śiva cave at Kunnâṇḍârkôyil (Pudukkottai) which contains inscriptions (Nos. 347 and 348, *G.O.*, No. 1260, Aug. 25, 1915) of the same epoch.

CONCLUSION.

We believe, that, in the preceding pages, we have brought certain new elements to bear upon the study of Pallava monuments.

1° The discovery of Pallava antiquities at Panamalai, Armamalai, Kîlmâvilangai, Singaperumâlkôyil, Siṅgavaram, Mêlachêri etc., has enlarged the field of investigation.

2° The antiquities already known have been studied with greater attention.

(*a*) From an epigraphical point of view we have closely examined the form of the various alphabets and we have brought to light certain inscriptions that still remain unpublished.

(*b*) From an archæological point of view we have tried to compose monographs of the most important monuments. We have given the plan of the temples and facsimiles of the photographs hitherto unpublished. Up to the present not a single book containing pictures of the monuments of Vallam, Dalavânûr, Mahêndravâḍi, Maṇḍagappattu, etc., has been published; and we think that the sculptures of the epoch of Mahêndra are so important for the history of art that they cannot be allowed to remain unknown any longer.

3° For the first time, we have made a general study of Pallava Antiquities based on a comparison of all the inscriptions and sculptures.

What then is the result of all this labour?

(*A*) Comparing the tenor of the inscriptions with the form of the sculptures, we have remarked that the monuments containing the inscriptions of a king called Mahêndra, Guṇabhara, Śatrumalla, Lalitaṅkura, belong to the same group by the similarity of their sculptures; and we have given to this kind of architecture the name "style of Mahêndra."

On the contrary, all the monuments bearing the inscriptions of Râjasiṁha have a very peculiar and characteristic style.

So the style of the sculptures accords with the tenor of the inscriptions.

But the form of the letters of the alphabets accords neither with the tenor of the inscriptions nor with the style of the monuments.

Thence, we have come to the conclusion that the form of the alphabet is not an absolute test for the determination of the age of antiquities and that inscriptions which, by their alphabets, seem to belong to different epochs, can, in reality, be contemporaneous.

(*B*) This comparative study of the collection of Pallava monuments has enabled us to try to compose a history of these antiquities of which a summary is given below:

It would appear that in the first centuries of our era, Hindu temples were built of wood and brick which are not very durable materials, and that is why we do not find their ruins anywhere. The antiquities in the caverns such as we have discovered at Kilaṅguṇam, Mâmbalappattu, Kâvakkâḍu, Armamalai, are the only vestiges of this epoch.

About the end of the VI century a taste for rock-cut temples spread everywhere in the Pallava kingdom.

The most ancient shrine of this kind is perhaps the small cave at Kîlmâvilaṅgai. The temple of Koranganimuttam is undoubtedly very old also.

The King Mahêndravarman I, who reigned at the beginning of the VII century (about 600–625), excavated the "caves" of Vallam, Mahêndravâdi, Pallâvaram, Trichinopoly. It is certainly at the same epoch that they cut in the rock the temples of Singavaram, Maṇḍagappattu, Tirukkalukkunram, Śîyamaṅgalam, Mâmandûr, Dalavânûr. It is not, however, improbable that some of them, for example, those at Singavaram and Śîyamaṅgalam, should have been hollowed out of the rock by Siṁhavishṇu, father of Mahêndravarman I.

The monuments of the time of Mahêndra are all of them "caves" excavated in the rock. The pillars are formed of two cubical parts separated by a prismatic part. The dvârapâlas present the front view and have very characteristic poses.

Narasiṁhavarman I. (Vâtâpikoṇḍa), who lived in the second quarter of the VII century (about 625–650), founded the town of Mahàbalipuram, to which he gave the name of Mâmallapuram, after his surname of Mâmalla, and had the "Rathas", the "Caves" and the large high reliefs "Kṛishṇa uplifting the Govardhana mountain" and "Bhâgîratha's penance" carved in the rock.

The monuments of Mahābalipuram very much resemble those of the epoch of Mahêndra. However the general aspect of the sculptures is altered. We get only side-views of the dvârapalas who have different poses. The elegant pillars with bulbous capitals take the place of the heavy pillars with cubical capitals. Lastly, these pillars are very often supported by squatting lions, which is a design never seen in any of the monuments of the time of Mahêndra. The squatting lion should have been an innovation of the artists of Mahābalipuram.

Paramêśvaravarman I. continued some of the works and had inscriptions engraved in them. He had to struggle hard against the Chalukyas about the year 660 or 670 A.D., and it is probable that during this time the works at Mahabalipuram were abandoned.

At the beginning of the VIII century, there appeared the new fashion of building temples entirely of stone and it is then (from about 700 to 710) that Rājasiṁha built the temples of Panamalai, Kailâsanâtha at Kañchîpuram, "Shore Temple" at Mahābalipuram, etc.

The mode of decoration also changed. Squatting lions continued to be sculptured for supporting the pillars; but for supporting the pilasters, they used rearing lions.

This new style continued to be used during the time of King Paramêśvaravarman II, who founded the Vaikuṇtha Perumal temple at Kâñchîpuram and of Nandivarmạn Pallavamalla.

The Pallava art, which reached its zenith at the time of Narasiṁhavarman I. (caves and rathas of Mahābalipuram), began to decline at the epoch of Râjasiṁha, and this decadence continued during the reign of the kings of the dynasty of Nandivarman.

G. JOUVEAU-DUBREUIL.

Pondicherry, June 29, 1916.

PALLAVA ANTIQUITIES

PALLAVA ANTIQUITIES

G. JOUVEAU-DUBREUIL

TRANSLATED INTO ENGLISH BY

V.S. SWAMINADHA DIKSHITAR

IN TWO VOLUMES
Vol. II

(With 8 Plates)

Published by

Facsimile Publisher
12 Pragati Market
Ashok Vihar, Ph-2
Delhi-110052
facsimilepublisher.com

Distribution Network
gyanbooks.com
India, USA, Canada, UK, Australia, France

ISBN : 978-93-5324-413-2 (Set)
ISBN : 978-93-5324-415-6 Vol. 2 (HB)
First Published, Pondicherry, 1918

2nd Impression 2020

Printed at: Gyan Press, Delhi.

Pallava Antiquities
Author: G. Jouveau-Dubreuil

PALLAVA ANTIQUITIES.

BY

G. JOUVEAU - DUBREUIL,
Doctor of the University of Paris,
Professor, College, Pondicherry.

VOL. II.

(*With 8 Plates*)

TRANSLATED INTO ENGLISH

BY

V. S. SWAMINADHA DIKSHITAR, B.A., L.T.,
Officier d'Académie
Professor of English, Colonial College, Pondicherry.

PONDICHERRY :
SOLD BY THE TRANSLATOR
32, Perumal Covil Street.

1918

PREFACE.

The author of this work, having been called to serve in the army and being therefore obliged to leave India shortly, regrets that Vol. II of "Pallava Antiquities" stands, owing to force of circumstances, reduced to a few pages.

I have, however, thought it necessary to publish it, because a study of the antiquities of the dynasty of Nandivarman constitutes an essential part of the work I have undertaken. We do not, in fact, know of any Pallava antiquity anterior to the year 600 A.D. As the Pallavas were succeeded by the Chôḷas only about 900, the Pallava Antiquities belong to the period between A.D. 600 and 900. And in Vol. I of "Pallava Antiquities," we have spoken only of the antiquities that belong to the first half of this period, that is, A.D. 600 to 750. What was then the nature of Pallava art in the second half of the above period, *i.e.*, from 750 to 900? That is the question we have treated in this book.

I must here inform the reader, that, during the year that has passed since the publication of Vol. I of this work, I have written two small books which, I think, must be read in order to understand this one.

In my work on "Dravidian Architecture," (edited with Preface and Notes by S. Krishnaswami Aiyangar, Professor, Madras University; printed at the S. P. C. K. Press, Vepery, Madras, 1917) I have tried to show the place occupied by the Pallava art in the general evolution of South Indian Architecture.

In "The Pallavas" (Pondicherry, 1917) I have tried to co-ordinate all that we know concerning the Pallavas with a view to establishing a complete genealogy of those kings and giving the outlines of their history.

Vol. II of "Pallava Antiquities" forms a necessary complement to those researches.

I take this occasion to thank M. R. Ry. V. S. Swaminatha Dikshitar who has done the translation, as well as Rev. Brother Joseph and Rev. Brother Paul of the Society of Jesus, who kindly had the book printed at the St. Joseph's Industrial School Press, Trichinopoly.

I wish, that, when the success of our arms would have brought us a glorious peace, I could return to India to continue these studies that are so dear to me.

PONDICHERRY,
30th December 1917.

G. JOUVEAU - DUBREUIL.

CHAPTER I.

THE ANTIQUITIES OF THE DYNASTY OF NANDIVARMAN.

In Vol. I of 'Pallava Antiquities,' I have studied exclusively the antiquities that could be attributed to the epoch of the dynasty of Siṁhavishṇu. It was then admitted that the fall of the dynasty of Siṁhavishṇu had produced a great anarchy in the Pallava empire and that a new dynasty, that of the Gaṅga-Pallavas, profited by these disturbances and gradually preponderated; Nandivarman Pallavamalla had a short and troublous reign and his successors were deprived of almost all the patrimony of the Pallavas. The Gaṅga-Pallava epoch extends from the death of Pallavamalla to the conquest of Âditya, but our knowledge of its history was very small. This period (from 750 to 900 A.D.), of a century and a half (the second half of the eighth and the whole of the ninth century) is the Gaṅga-Pallava epoch; and in a work devoted to the Pallavas the question of the Gaṅga-Pallava antiquities did not arise.

I have shown in my book "The Pallavas" that the Vâyalûr inscription proves that the Gaṅga-Pallava theory is false and that we must admit the theory of M. R. Ry. T. A. Gopinatha Rao, according to which the so-called Gaṅga-Pallavas were only the Pallavas of the dynasty of Nandivarman.

Contrary to what has been believed up to the present, these princes were powerful and glorious. Their empire extended from Kâḷahasti in the north to Pudukôṭṭa in the south and they had contended, many a time, victoriously, against the Pâṇḍyas.

From an architectural point of view, it is specially interesting to study this epoch as it forms the transition period between the Siṁhavishṇu and the Chôḷa dynasties: in Vol. I of " Pallava Antiquities " we have studied the style of Râjasiṁha which dates from about 700 A.D. Besides, in my work on " Dravidian Architecture," I have given a description of the temple of Dâdâpuram (*Vide* Dravidian Architecture, fig. 26) which contains an inscription of Râjarâja and can be considered as a good type of the " Early Chôḷa " style at the end of the X century. It was therefore necessary to define exactly the style that was employed at the end of the Pallava period; so, I asked myself: " Which are the temples that date from the dynasty of Nandivarman, that is, from 720 to 900? " and it is this important question that I propose to handle.

We shall divide the subject into two parts: I. Antiquities that do not bear any inscriptions of the dynasty of Nandivarman; II. Antiquities bearing inscriptions of that dynasty.

Section I. Antiquities without inscriptions.

A) Certain temples that do not bear any Pallava inscription, perhaps belong to the time of the Nandivarman dynasty. Such are: the temple of Kailâsanâtha at Tiruppattûr (*Vide G. O.* No. 574, 17th July 1908.— Part II, No. 9, p. 60 and photos nos. 89 to 91 of Appendix

D); the Jain temple of Varthamânasvâmi at Tiruppa-ruttikunru near Conjeevaram, (Photos Nos. C. 27 and C. 28, Class C of the collections of Madras Archælogical Survey).

The maṇḍapam that is found before the cave dug in the rock at Śîyamaṅgalam is probably the one which, according to inscription No. 68 of 1900, was built in the 21st year of the reign of Nandivikramavarman. However since the inscription is not engraved on the maṇḍapam, but on the rock of the cave built by Mahêndravarman I, one cannot be positive about the date of this building.

In this list, I would place the Kailâsanâthâ temple at Uttaramallûr. This temple is almost entirely built of brick and bears only one inscription of Râjêndra-Chôḷa (No. 56 of 1898). But when I visited Uttaramallûr, I discovered that the above temple belongs to a style much anterior to that of the time of Râjêndra Chôḷa and can be put in the category of Pallava temples. However, owing to the uncertainty of the age of these temples, none of them can be taken as typical of the style of the dynasty of Nandivarman.

B) A few temples do not probably belong to the Pallava period, though certain marks would lead us to think otherwise.

The temple of Pallavanêśvara at Pallavanêśvaram (Śâyâvanam) near Kâvirippaṭṭiṉam is not a Pallava structure as one might belive judging from its name.

The temple of Kailâsanâtha at Âlambâkkam founded by Dantivarman (*G. O.* No. 665, 28th July 1910, Part II, No. 7, p. 71) was probably rebuilt during the Chôḷa period (*Vide* photo No. 14, *G. O.* No. 665, 28th July 1910, Appendix D, pago 62).

There is, in the village of Ukkal, a temple containing very ancient Chôḷa inscriptions in which the village is called Aparâjita-Chaturvêdimaṅgalam; one may therefore believe that the temple is of the time of the Pallava king Aparâjita. I therefore went to see this temple and found that the major portion of it had disappeared. There yet remains only the lower portion which is covered with inscriptions but is not at all an interesting piece of architecture.

The temple of Chandramauḷiśvara at Brahmadêśam, which, M. R. Ry. H. Krishna Sastri says (Report for 1916, Part II, No. 8), is probably a Pallava one, is in reality a fine specimen of the "Early Chôḷa" style.

Lastly, the temple of Veṅkatêsa - Perumal, which, M. R. Ry. H. Krishna Sastri says "must be traced to the time of the Gaṅga-Pallava king Nṛipatuṅga," does not surely belong to that epoch, as I have been able to ascertain during my visit to that place.

Section II. Antiquities with inscriptions.

A) A few antiquities contain inscriptions of the dynasty of Nandivarman, but they are not written in the alphabet of that period and are therefore only copies; they are the following: No. 1, a of 1890 (Nṛipatuṅga, 17th year); Nos. 460 and 461 of 1905 (Nṛipatuṅga, 11th and 15th years); No. 199 of 1907 (Nandi), No. 48 of 1914 (Nandi, 22nd year). The inscriptions No. 150 of 1916 at Poyyanur and No. 152 of 1916 at Kîlpulam which are dated in the 2nd year of the reign of Vayiramêga, have been attributed to the Pallavas (Report for 1916, Part II, No. 7, p. 115). However, the alphabet of these inscriptions is almost modern and it is not possible to date them in the time of the dynasty of Nandivarman.

B) Certain inscriptions are engraved on unsculptured rocks; they are: No. 76 of 1889; No. 10 of 1895; No. 304 of 1897; No. 73 of 1900; Nos. 295, 296, 297, 300, 302, and 303 of 1902; No. 529 of 1905; No. 82 of 1908; No. 88 of 1910; No. 283 of 1916,

These inscriptions are useful only from a historical point of view and in no way help the archæologist in the discovery of Pallava monuments. We must however make an exception in the case of inscription No. 529 of 1905 which is engraved on the rock by the side of the Śiva Temple, at Tiruvaḷḷaṟai, that is cut in the same rock. We may therefore presume that both the cave and the inscription are contemporaneous, without however being quite sure of it.

I have visited this spot. The cave is very simple, destitute of ornamentation and does not offer much architectural interest; it may be attibuted to the same epoch as the inscription, that is, to the reign of Dantivarman.

C) A very large number of inscriptions are of no use to the archæologist, as they are engraved either on isolated stones or on stones that have been used in the reconstruction of buildings. In the latter case the edifice is not of the same date as the inscription. Such are: Nos. 27, 54 and 55 of 1887; 12 of 1895; 7 and 8 of 1896; 11 and 17 of 1899; 226, 228, 229 and 234 of 1903; 262 of 1904; 394 and 397 of 1905; 180 of 1907; 68, 351 and 352 of 1908; 349 of 1911; 31, 32, 158, 159, 161, 162, 163, 180, 190, 257 and 417 of 1912; 179 of 1915; and an inscription of Nandippôttaraśar at Mallam registered in 1908.

We may place in this category inscription No. 541 of 1905 which is engraved on a well at Tiruvellarai ; this well has however been repaired either before or during the year 1262-63 (*G. O.* No. 492, 2nd July 1906, Part II, No. 4, page 62).

We have mentioned in the above list only those inscriptions that are distinctly stated in the Reports on Epigraphy to have been engraved either on detached stones (slabs) or on stones built into a more modern wall (stone built into the wall).

D) Some inscriptions are engraved on Pallava temples that bear some ancient inscriptions of the Simhavishṇu dynasty.

Inscriptions 68 of 1900 and 49 of 1905 are engraved on the caves of Śîyamaṅgalam and Dalavânûr, which we have attributed in Vol. I of "Pallava Antiquities" to king Mahêndravarman I of the dynasty of Simhavishṇu.

We have spoken in page 44 of "The Pallavas" of the Śiva temple at Kuram and attributed its foundation to king Paramêśvaravarman I. This temple was therefore in existence when inscriptions Nos. 37 and 38 of 1900 were engraved during the reigns of Nandivarman and Nṛipatuṅga.

Inscriptions 35 and 36 of 1903 are found at the entrance to the sanctuary of Vîraṭṭaṇêśvara temple at Tiruvadi; in page 46 of our work, "The Pallavas," we have said that this temple which contains an inscription of Paramêśvaravarman could be attributed to Paramêśvaravarman II of the dynasty of Simhavishṇu.

E) In certain temples we find inscriptions of the Nandivarman dynasty, written in ancient characters, which give no information at all concerning the building of the monuments bearing them. Such are: 84 of

1892; 14 of 1893; 17 and 52 of 1895; 51, 61, 64, 65, 72, 74, 80, 81, 82 and 83 of 1898; 33 and 35 of 1900; 283, 300, 301 and 303 of 1901; 220, 277 and 278 of 1902; 404, and 406 of 1905; 347 and 348 of 1914.

None of the monuments containing these inscriptions can be—strictly speaking—taken as types of the art during the epoch of the dynasty of Nandivarman, as the building of the temple is not mentioned in the inscription. However, some of these temples are built by the Pallavas and we must say a few words about them.

I visited the Jain temple of Rishabanâtha at Perumaṇḍûr (near Tindivaṇam—South Arcot District), from which, inscription No. 220 of 1902 has been copied. Though I searched, I have not been able to find any trace of Pallava style in this place.

I went to Uttaramallûr (15 miles west of Chingleput) where there are two temples containing Pallava inscriptions. The temple of Vaikuṇṭha Perumal, with its 9 Pallava inscriptions (Nos. 61, 64, 65, 72, 74, 80, 81, 82, 83 of 1898), first attracts our attention. Unfortunately, this temple is not at all interesting from an architectural point of view. A portion of the temple has been rebuilt and the old walls that remain are but the basements without any style.

The temple of Sundaravarada-Perumal that contains but one inscription (No. 51 of 1898) is much more interesting and can surely be classed among the Pallava temples. Unfortunately, most of the buildings are made of brick and covered with lime.

The temple of Kôviladi, between Tanjore and Trichinopoly, in which inscriptions Nos. 283, 300, 301 and 303 of 1901 are engraved, is in ruins.

The temple of Kîlur (suburb of Tirukoilur) which contained inscriptions Nos. 277 and 278 of 1902 was completely rebuilt about 10 years ago. When I visited this place, I found the remains of this ancient temple lying on the banks of the Pennar and, from the scattered stones, I was able to ascertain that it was a very fine temple that had been destroyed.

The Muktêśvara temple at Conjeevaram which contains an inscription of Nandivarman (No. 14 of 1893) probably belongs to the time of Nandivarman Pallavamalla. The style of it which can be discerned from plates XVIII and XIX of Mr. A. Rea's "Pallava Architecture" resembles that of the temples of Râjasiṁha and we may affirm that this monument belongs to the first half of the VIII century.

Mr. A. Rea has said in page 46 of his "Pallava Architecture" that the Perumâl temple at Kûram is « a very doutful specimen, and, if in reality Pallava, must be one of the very latest examples ». I do not think so: the temple of Kêsavaperumâḷ at Kûram is certainly in the style of Râjasiṁha: besides, there is on the southern side of it, an inscription (No. 35 of 1900) dated in the 12th year of the reign of Dantivarman and there is no doubt that this temple belongs to the second half of the VIII century. A plan of this temple is given in Plate CXXI of Mr. A. Rea's "Pallava Architecture". Inscription No. 33 of 1900 was engraved in this temple at the time of Nṛipatuṅga.

The rock-cut temple at Kunnâṇḍâr Koil (Pudukottai State) which contains inscriptions Nos. 346, 347 and 348 of 1914 probably belongs to the VIII century.

I have visited the rock-cut shrine enclosed in the Vishṇu temple at Tiruvellarai which bears inscription

No. 537 of 1905 on one of its pillars. It is left unfinished and is not interesting.

In "Pallava Antiquities" Vol. I., I have spoken about the Mataṇgêsvara temple at Kâñchîpuram. This temple « which belongs to the style of Râjasiṁha (*Vide* » Pallava Architecture, by Alexander Rea, Madras, » 1909), can be ascribed to the end of the VIII century. » It must be specially mentioned that the temple of » Mataṇgêsvara contains dvârapâlas having four hands » (*Vide* A. Rea: Pallava Architecture, Pl. XLV.) We » have already said that the dvârapâlas of the Pallava » period have only two hands. This exception seems » to prove that the temple of Mataṇgêśvara belongs to » the end of the Pallava period.»

In the course of this year (1917), I discovered an inscription which has not been mentioned by any one till now.

The inscription is on one of the two pillars which are inside the temple.

I read the word: श्री अरत्यकन Śrî Aratyakana in Pallava-Grantha characters. The letters are so formed that we may say that the inscription belongs to the VIII century. So, we must attribute the Matañgês-vara temple at Kâñchîpuram to king Nandivarman Pallavamalla.

F) There are only three temples that contain inscriptions which show plainly that they have been built in the period of the dynasty of Nandivarman.

They are:

1° The Śiva temple at Malayadippatti (Pudukkôṭṭai State) which was cut in the rock in the 16th year of the reign of Dantivarman (Journal of the South Indian

Association, July 1911, Vol. II, No. 1, page 22, Some inscriptions of the Muttaraiyars, by T. A. Gopinatha Rao—inscriptions Nos. III and IV).

2° The Śiva temple at Nârthâmalai (Pudukkôṭṭai State) which was cut in the rock in the 7th year of the reign of Nṛipatuṅga (insc. No. 365 of 1904).

3° The temple of Vîraṭṭaṉêśvara at Tiruttaṇi which was built by Nambi Appi, a contemporary of the Pallava king, Aparâjita (insc. Nos. 433 and 435 of 1905).

The Śiva temple at Malayaḍippaṭṭi is a small rock-cut temple containing two cubical pillars at the façade, a verandah and a sanctuary with a liṅgam in it.

The Śiva temple at Nârthâmalai is in ruins.

We shall not now make a special study of the temples of Malaiyaḍippatti and Nârthâmalai for the following reasons:

a) Strictly speaking, these monuments are not the work of the Pallavas, but, of the Muttaraiyars who chose to depend on the Pallavas or the Pâṇḍyas according to the freaks of the politics of the day.

b) These caves belong, by their architecture, to the group of caves dug under the initiative of the Pâṇḍya kings. [For instance, we know that the Aṉamalai cave was dug in 769 during the reign of the Pâṇḍya king, Jatila Parantaka.]

M. R. Ry. K. Venkatarangam, curator of the Pudukkôṭṭai museum, intends to give in his Bulletin a detailed description of these temples.

We shall therefore take up now for our study only one temple, that of Aparâjita at Tiruttaṇi, which, as we shall see, is highly interesting.

Plate I.

The Virattanêsvara temple at Tiruttani.

Plate II.

Upper part of the façade of the pallava temple at Tiruttani.

CHAPTER II.

THE TEMPLE OF VÎRATTANESVARA AT TIRUTTANI.

The inscription No. 433 of 1905 engraved on the southern wall of the "vimâna" of Vîraṭṭanêśvara temple at Tiruttaṇi is a Tamil verse (Veṇbâ) which says that the temple in question was built of granite by a certain Nambi-Appi. The verse is said to have been composed by the king whose name is not given; but inscription No. 435 of 1905 engraved on the same wall mentions a donation made to the temple by the same Nambi-Appi in the 18th year of the reign of Aparâjita Vikramavarman (*G. O.* No. 492, 2nd July 1906, Part II, No. 8, page 64). It must also be said that the two inscriptions (Nos. 433 and 435) are written in the same alphabet which is that of the end of the IX century.

We know for certain the date of the reign of Aparâjita, as the Udayendiram plates (*G.O.* No. 492, 2nd July 1906, page 64) say that this king was the ally of Pṛithivîpathi I. against Varaguṇa Pâṇḍya about the year 879; besides, we learn from the Tiruvâlaṅgâḍu plates (Report for 1906, page 65) that the Chôḷa king Âditya I, having defeated Aparâjita, seized the Pallava empire, and we also know that this conquest was made before A.D. 900. We may therefore affirm that the temple of Vîraṭṭanêśvara at Tiruttani was built in the last quarter of the IX century.

The inscriptions in the temple were copied by M.R.Ry. K. V. Subrahmaniya Aiyar about the end of August 1905, and V Venkayya has given an account of them in his report on Epigraphy for 1905-06. But, while the historical importance of the inscriptions at Tiruttaṇi has been known for the last twelve years, the importance of the temple from an architectural point of view has been completely ignored up to the present day.

The report on Epigraphy says nothing about this style of architecture. No photographs of the temple have been taken either by the Epigraphical or the Archæological Department. No one has spoken in any work about the architecture of this temple. Lastly, even in the list of ancient monuments preserved by the Archæological Department, we do not find any mention of the temple of Vîraṭṭanêśvara.

Now we have to solve the following question: Is the present temple the same as the one built by Nambi-Appi at the time of Aparâjita? Has it lasted a thousand years without undergoing any alteration or repair?

To be able to answer this question, I went to Tiruttaṇi in January 1917, and discovered that the present temple has remained marvellously intact and that, from top to bottom, it has not undergone any repair; being built entirely of granite, it has successfully resisted the ravages of centuries and appears to be almost new, though from the details of its architecture and ornamentation, we recognise it to be an excellent type of Pallava Art.

This temple is the only specimen we have of a Pallava monument belonging to the end of the IX century whose architectural style is excellent and whose age has been correctly fixed by the inscriptions.

Plate III.

The Pallava temple at Tiruttani. (Northern side.)

Plate IV.

Image of Kâli, on the northern side of the pallava temple at Tiruttani.

I therefore propose to take the temple of Vîraṭṭanêśvara at Tiruttaṇi as the type of a temple belonging to the end of the Pallava period.

It is very easy to visit the Pallava temple at Tiruttaṇi. This town is a station on the railway line between Arkonam and Renigunta. It is the first station after Arkonam from where it can be reached in a few minutes. There may be some difficulty in finding this Pallava temple as it is one of the most modest of all the temples there. Our temple is to the east of the railway station. At a short distance to the east of the station, there is a small river and the temple stands amidst trees on the other side of the river.

The plan of the temple is very simple. It is a vimâna 4½ yards square, in the middle of which there is a chamber (Garbhagṛaham) containing the liṅgam. This chamber has no windows but has only one doorway facing east.

In front of this doorway there is a small maṇḍapam without windows but with a door on the east side.

Thus, the temple is so placed that the entrance faces the rising sun.

The base of the vimâna is square, but the upper portion presents a peculiarity which M. R. Ry. T. A. Gopinatha Rao has described (Five Bâna Inscriptions at Gudimallam, *Indian Antiquary*, 1911) under the name of "Gajapṛishṭhâkṛiti shape".

In other words, the upper portion is apsidal and its form recalls to our mind the Sahadeva Ratha at Mahâbalipuram.

I request the reader to compare Plate I of this book with figure 193 in "*History of Indian and Eastern Architecture* by Ferguson and Burgess" 1910 Edition, vol. I, page 337. It will be found that the upper portion of the Tiruttaṇi temple resembles very much the Sahâdêva Ratha at Mahâbalipuram. I must also state that the stone elephant found in the midst of the Rathas of Mahâbalipuram is placed close to Sahâdêva Ratha in such a manner that it would appear that the Pallava sculptors of Mahâbalipuram wanted to draw the attention of the on-lookers to the elephantine form of the Ratha.

We have said in our work "*The Pallavas*" (page 45) that the Śiva temple at Kûram which was built in the reign of Paramêśvaravarman I. is also apsidal in form.

Burgess (*Indian and Eastern Architecture*, vol. I, edition of 1910, pages 127 and 336) has shown that this form was copied from that of the Buddhist Chaityas which are also apsidal in shape. Some of these Chaityas have been adapted to the cult of the liṅgam on account of the resemblance between the Buddhist dâgoba and the liṅgam. That is why the apsidal temples are a speciality of the cult of the liṅgam as has been observed by M. R. Ry. T. A. Gopinatha Rao in the above mentioned article.

The temple of Kapôtêśvara at Chezarla is an example of the adaptation of the Chaityas to the cult of the liṅgam. If we bear in mind that Chezarla (Chêjerla) is in the Narasaraopet Taluq of the Guntur district, the same Taluq in which have been discovered the plates of Maidavôlu, Darśi, Narasaraopet, that is, in the centre of the Pallava kingdom, it would appear quite natural that the Pallavas should adopt this kind of architecture.

The façade of the Chaityas is ornamented with gables having the form of a horse-shoe (horse-shoe-shaped façade) which is well known to the archæologists. At

Tiruttaṇi, we find (*vide* Plate II) a similar horse-shoe; only the upper portion is different : instead of the shovel-head of the Kûdus of Mahâbalipuram we find the huge head of a lion (Siṁha).

As at Mahâbalipuram, the central portion contains an edifice; the one at Tiruttaṇi contains an image (*vide* Plate II) of Śiva and Parvati which reminds us of the images of Somaskanda which became so numerous during the time of Râjasiṁha.

Thus the upper portion of the Tiruttaṇi temple is a very curious and interesting piece of architecture.

The lower portion also presents a character which is completely peculiar to the Pallava style: the corbels which are above the capitals have a curved profile. I have said in my "*Dravidian Architecture*," page 28: « It is necessary, however, to remark that the circular form (No. 2 of fig. 20) was peculiar to the Pallava epoch.»

We see that we were quite right in saying so, since we find that Aparâjita's temple at Tiruttaṇi which belongs to the end of the Pallava period still contains corbels having a curved profile.

Plate V is intended to draw the attention of the reader to this important *motif* of ornamentation which is not so well seen in Plates III and IV. The corbel at Tiruttaṇi, *vide* Plate V, No. II, is absolutely identical with that of the temple of Râjasiṁha at Panamalai (vide *Pallava Antiquities*, vol. I, Plate III.)

It is necessary to insist on the great importance of this detail, for, this curved form of the corbel seems to disappear with the Pallava dynasty and all the "Early Chôḷa" temples have angular corbels similar to the one we have represented in fig. 27 of "*Dravidian Architecture*"

The Kûdu at Tiruttaṇi has not the shovel-head which is found in the most ancient Pallava temples, but we see, in its place, the head of a lion.

Lastly, it must also be said that we do not find anywhere the rearing lions that characterise the art of Râjasiṁha.

From an iconographical point of view the Vîrattaṇêśvara temple at Tiruttaṇi presents certain peculiarities.

The sanctuary contains a liṅgam which is not prismatic and in the wall, at the back of the sanctuary, there is no image of Somaskanda.

Plate VI, which is the reproduction of a photograph taken with magnesium light, will enable us to see distinctly the liṅgam and the back of the sanctuary in the temple at Tiruttaṇi.

The two Dvârapâlas on each side of the entrance (*vide* also Pl. VI) have an extremely characteristic pose which recalls to our mind the poses of the glorious epoch of the Pallavas; they have, however, unlike all others, four arms.

The four walls of the Vimâna are adorned with niches containing statues: In the south, Dakshiṇâmûrti; in the west, Vishṇu; in the north, Brahmâ. Besides this, the small maṇḍapam which forms an antechamber at the entrance of the temple is ornamented in the south with a niche containing Gaṇêśa and in the north with one containing Kâli.

Plates IV, VII and VIII show the form of these statues.

The image of Dakshiṇâmûrti (Plate VII) is absolutely identical with the one that M. R. Ry. T. A. Gopinatha Rao has described in Vol. II, Part I,

Plate V.

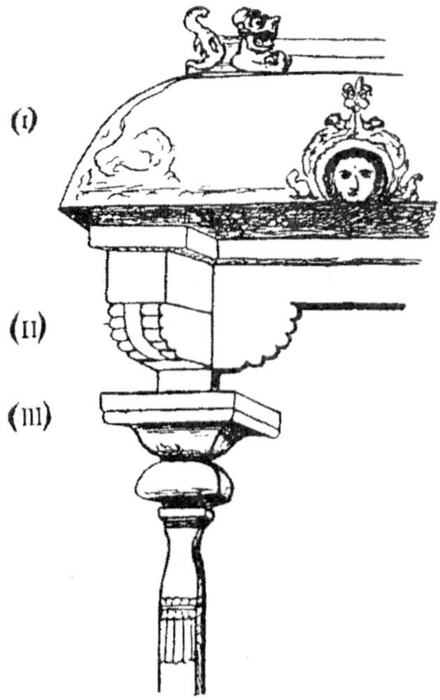

Pallava style at Tiruttani :

(I) The larmier (Kabôdam).

(II) The corbel.

(III) The abacus (Palagi).

Plate VI.

Dvârapâlas at Tiruttani. (Virattanesvara temple.)

pages 282 and 283 of his book in the following terms :
« Fig. 2, Plate LXXIV is the photograph of the
» figure of Dakshinâmûrti found in Kâvêripakkam
» and belongs to the Pallava period. Herein, the deity
» has on his head heavy curls of hair constituting
» the jaṭâbhâra; he carries the akshamâlâ in his back
» right hand, agni (?) in the back left hand, and a
» book in the front left hand; the front right hand
» is held in the Vyâkhyâna-mudrâ pose. The right
» leg is hanging below the seat, while the left one is
» kept bent in the utkuṭikâsana posture. Round the
» neck are two hârâs (necklaces) on the chest, the
» Yajñopavîta and in one ear a vṛittakuṇḍala; the
» other ear wears no ornament. Below the seat are to
» be seen a deer and a cobra listening to his discourse.»

Relying on the form of the statue, Mr. Gopinatha Rao thinks that it "belongs to the Pallava period" and this supposition is now confirmed by a study of the temple built by Aparâjita at Tiruttaṇi.

The image of Vishṇu is distinguished by his insignia of Śaṅkha and Chakra which are ornamented with flames of fire. We know that these flames were introduced in iconography only at the time of Râjasiṁha (vide *Pallava Antiquities*, vol. I, page 58). At Tiruttaṇi, the Chakra of Vishṇu has the form of a cube and not that of a wheel. This curious sort of Chakra is found in Tondai-maṇḍalam in most of the temples built in the X century.

The image of Brahmâ presents a very remarkable peculiarity. The Brahmanical cord (Yajñôpavîta) does not fall on the right hip but passes over the right arm. The same peculiarity is seen in the images of Vishṇu and the Dvârapâlakas; but this detail is almost invisible in Plates VI and VII; on the contrary, in Plate VIII which represents Brahmâ, we see very well the Yajñôpavîta passing over the right arm. This peculiarity is a characteristic sign of archaism. It is frequently met with in ancient sculptures.

If the reader looks at fig. B of Plate XXVI of Vol. I of *Pallava Antiquities*, he will find there a Dvârapâla of the cave at Tirukkalukkunram. This Dvârapâla holds up his right arm and we see very clearly the Yajñôpavîta placed over this arm. In Plate XXVIII we see very well the Yajñôpavîta of the right Dvârapâla in the rock-cut temple at Mandagapaṭṭu thrown over his right arm. Thus, then, this mode existed even at the time of Aparâjita, i.e., about 880. It completely disappeared afterwards.

Kâli (*vide* Plate IV) bears the Śaṅka and Chakra which are identical with those we have just described in connection with Vishṇu.

We believe we have proved by what has been said above that the temple of Virattanêsvara at Tiruttaṇi is extremely interesting owing to its architecture as well as its iconography. From it, we obtain a correct knowledge of Pallava Art as it existed a little before the conquest of Tondai-maṇḍalam by Aditya Chôḷa.

We have said at the beginning of this chapter that king Aparâjita composed the Tamil verse that commemorates the building of this temple by Nambi-Appi. The Tiruttaṇi temple was thus built under the patronage of the Pallava king and also inaugurated by him. I therefore think of giving the name of the last of the Pallavas to the last style of Pallava architecture and therefore call the style of the Tiruttaṇi temple " the style of Aparâjita."

Plate VII.

(I) Śiva. (II) Ganeśha. (III) Vishṇu.

Images on the southern and western side of the pallava temple at Tiruttaṇi.

Plate VIII.

Brahma.

(Tiruttani.—Northern side of the pallava temple.)

CONCLUSION.

It is now possible for us to give the history of South Indian Art from the remotest times to the tenth century.

The art of writing was known from the time of Aśôka, as the caverns in the province of Madura, which were occupied by Buddhist and Jain monks, contain inscriptions in Brahmi written in the same Alphabet as those of Aśôka. The beds of the Pâṇḍavas, which are seen in such large numbers in the Gingee hills, belong probably to this epoch. In this connection, I would mention some antiquities of this kind which I have not seen mentioned in any other book. In the enclosure of the Jain temple of Appandanandar at Tirunirankonrai, 12 miles south-east of Tirukkôyilûr, there is a very curious cavern which contains very remarkable beds.

Śivaism flourished at the same time, as is proved by the remarkable liṅgam discovered by M. R. Ry. T. A. Gopinatha Rao at Gudimallam (*Elements of Hindu Iconography* by T. A. Gopinatha Rao, Vol. II, Part I, Plates II, III, IV and V), which probably belongs to the period anterior to the Christian era.

I do not not think it necessary to recount here the story of King Chenkuttuvan, who built a temple for Kannagi, probably in the second century after Christ. If we bear in mind that there was, at this epoch, a temple of Augustus on the Malabar Coast and that the sculptures of Ceylon and Amaravati were all Roman in workmanship, we may suppose that the statues of this period—perhaps even the statue of Kannagi, which under the orders of Chenkuttuvan was made of a piece of stone brought from Northern India — were made of white marble and in the Roman style. M. R. Ry. T. A. Gopinatha Rao has, besides, discovered, in the innermost prakaram of the Kamatchiamman temple at Kâñchîpuram, a statue of Buddha, which is in what is called the "Græco-Buddhist" style and which probably belongs to the second or the third century (*Ind. Ant.*, Vol. XLIV, Part DLVII, June 1915).

Be that as it may, we may say that, up to the end of the VI century, South India, which possessed already a very ancient and splendid civilisation, did not yet see the birth of its art. The temples were built of materials which were not durable, and the artists did not at all care to make stone carvings to honour their gods: and there are no antiquities belonging to this epoch.

The birth of this art took place during the reign of the Pallava Kings of the dynasty of Siṁhavishṇu, for reasons which we shall now explain.

There was a great revival of letters and arts in Northern India towards the fifth century. The renaissance of the sculptural art manifested itself in the form of rock-cut temples It was because Buddhism with the doctrine of Mahayana was still in the plenitude of its power and the monks have always had the habit of excavating their monasteries on the side of the mountains.

It is at this time that the rock of Ajaṇṭâ—which for a long time had been dug in by the Buddhists—was embellished with new hypogeums which display all the luxury of decoration which is a wonder to modern archæologists. We owe these works to the princes of the dynasty of Vâkâtakas. Inscriptions Nos. 622 and 624 in Keilhorn's list published in the report on the "Archæological Survey of Western India," IV, pp. 124 and 129, show that the caves Nos. 16 and 17 of Ajaṇtâ were dug during the reign of Harisheṇa of the Vâkâṭaka dynasty. For information about this dynasty we must read Vincent A. Smith's excellent article on "The Vâkâṭaka dynasty of Berar in the 4th and 5th centuries A.D.", which is published in "The journal of the Royal Asiatic Society, April 1914." In it the author has proved that King Harisheṇa reigned from about 465 to 500. The Ajaṇtâ inscriptions show that Harisheṇa extended his conquests over the following countries: Kuntala, Avanti, Kalinga, Kosala, Trikûta, Lâta and Ândhra. Mr. Vincent A. Smith has proved (page 330) that Kuntala comprised North Mysore, Chitaldrug and Bellary; Kalinga is the well-known province to the north of the Godavery by the Bay of Bengal.

Thus we learn from the Ajaṇtâ inscriptions that the king who dug the caves Nos. 16 and 17 extended his conquests over a part of the Telugu country not far from the mouth of the Godavery and the Krishṇâ.

The Vishṇukuṇḍins reigned over the kingdom of Vengi which was between these two rivers. Their capital was Lenduḷûru, now Dendulûru, which is a suburb of the town of Vengi. The Chikkula plates (*Ep. Ind.* Vol. IV, No. 25, p. 195) say that the Vishṇukuṇḍins reigned on the banks of the Krishṇâ. They also say that the birth of King Vikramêndravarman I. "was embellished by the two families of the Vishṇukuṇḍins and Vâkâtakas," that is to say, that the mother of the

Vishṇukuṇḍin King Vikramêndravarman I. was a Vâkâtaka princess. I shall here bring forward a proposition, which, I think, I am the first to do, and which will throw much light on the chronology of the Vishṇukuṇḍins: "The king Mâdhavavarman married toward the year 500 A.D. the daughter of Harisena and begot a son Vikramêndravarman I." This proposition is rendered highly probable by the fact that the Vâkâtakas reigned in Berar and that only Harisena who made conquests in the Deckan could have had relations with the Vishṇukuṇḍins who reigned near Bezwada. I think we can settle the chronology of the Vishṇukuṇḍins from that time as follows:

Mâdhavavarman (about 500)
|
Vikramêndravarman I. (about 530)
|
Indrabhattârakavarman (about 560)
|
Vikramêndravarman II. (about 590)

If therefore we find caves cut in the rocks on the banks of the Krishnâ, at Bezwada, Mogulrazapuram, Sittanagaram, Undavalli, there is nothing wonderful about it, since we now know that the Vishṇukuṇḍins who reigned in this region were related to the Vâkâtakas who reigned at Ajaṇtâ.

I do not think it necessary to repeat here what I have said in Chapter III of my work, "The Pallavas." When visiting the caves of Undavalli, I made the important discovery that their style was identical with the one that I have described in Vol. I. of "Pallava Antiquities" under the name of "The Style of Mahêndra." Besides, I have said that the presence, in the caves of Trichinopoly and Pallâvaram, of names of Telugu origin proves that their author Mahêndravarman I. was a native of the Telugu Country. The Vâyalûr inscription shows, in fact, that Mahêndravarman I. was the grandson of Vishṇugôpa of the Chûra plates, who reigned at Palakkada, that is to say, in the Telugu Country to the south of the Krishnâ. The same inscription also shows that Mahêndravarman I. is the first king of that name, and from that we have come to the conclusion that the mother of Mahêndravarman I. was a Vishṇukuṇḍin princess.

I believe that I have now explained how it is that, all of a sudden, at the begnining of the VII century, there spead in the Tamil Country the novel fashion of cutting caves in the rocks. The Pallava art came into existence from that circumstance.

The study that we have made in the first two volumes of "Pallava Antiquities" enables us to divide the history of Pallava Art into four periods of style of unequal duration :

(1) The style of Mahêndra, from 610 to 640.
(2) The style of Mâmalla, from 640 to 674.
(3) The style of Râjasiṁha, from 674 to 800.
(4) The style of Aparâjita, from 800 to 900.

It is necessary, however, to specify that this division of the Pallava art into four different styles applies only to the country lying immediately round the capital, Kâñchi, *i.e.* to Toṇḍaimaṇḍalam. If, in fact, we go farther from this region, for example, in the south, to the country between Tanjore and Pudukôttai, we do not find an exactly similar kind of evolution. This country over which the Muttaraiyars reigned has been under the influence of the Pâṇḍyas and the Chôḷas.

In the account that follows, we shall speak only of the architecture in Toṇḍaimaṇḍalam.

1° *The Style of Mahêndra.*

The discovery of the work called Mattavilâsaprahasana (Trivandram Sanskrit Series, No LV—edited by T. Ganapati Sâstri—Trivandram Government Press, 1917) and the discovery that this work is mentioned in the Mâmaṇḍûr inscriptions (see: "The Pallavas," chap. IV, pages 38 and 39), have left no room to doubt that it was Mahêndravarman I, son of Siṁhavishṇu, that was the author of the caves found at Vallam, Mahêndravâdi, Dalavânur, Śîyamangalam and Pallavaram.

These caves, which are all of them situated in Toṇḍaimaṇḍalam, are distinguished by 1° sanctuaries destitute of the image of Somaskanda, 2° circular liṅgams, 3° dvarapâlas of special forms, 4° double-arched Tiruvatchis (Toranas), and 5° cubical pillars; lastly, we have also to remark that they are all of them subterranean maṇḍapams.

2° *The Style of Mâmalla.*

We have proved (*Pallava Antiquities*, Vol. I, pages 57, 58, 59, 60) that the style of the Caves and the Rathas of Mahâbalipuram (Mâmallapuram) belongs exactly to the transition period between the styles of Mahêndra and Râjasiṁha. Now that we are sure that this Mahêndra is Mahêndravarman I, we can, without any hesitation, attribute the caves and rathas of Mahâbalipuram to the two kings that reigned between Mahêndravarman I. and Râjasiṁha; so, from an archæological point of view, we can be sure that the caves and the rathas of Mahâbalipuram were begun by Narasiṁhavarman I, surnamed Mâmalla, and continued by Paramêśvaravarman I. Most of these monuments remain unfinished, it would appear, owing to the invasion of the Châlukyas in A.D. 674.

In the style of Mâmalla, we begin to see the image of Somaskanda at the back of the Śiva shrines. The Dvârapâlas do not have the same pose as at the epoch of Mahêndra. It seems that it was at the time of Narasiṁhavarman I. (Mâmalla) that the Pallava artists who dug the rocks at Mahâbalipuram invented the system of making pillars with lions squatting at the base. This *motif* of ornamentation is not found either in the caves near Bezwada or in those of Mahêndra. I think that this *motif* was invented at Mahâbalipuram about the year 640. It is remarkable that the temples of this epoch consist not only of subterranean maṇḍapams but also of rathas, which shows that they had already an outward form, an external architecture.

3° *The Style of Râjasimha.*

At the time of Râjasiṁha, the sculptors were not content with having squatting lions, but put up a large number of rearing lions on the buildings. Prismatic lingams placed in front of the image of Somaskanda are now found in the sanctuaries. The Tiruvatchis (Toranas) are single-arched. Rock-cut temples become rare; the temples of this epoch are built of pieces of stone placed above one another.

King Narasiṁhavarman I. built the temples of Airavatêsvara (*vide* "The Pallavas," chap. IV, page 46) and Kailâsanatha at Kâñchîpuram, the shore temple at Mahâbalipuram and the temple at Panamalai. Paramêśvaravarman I. probably built the temple of Vîrattanêśvara at Tiruvadi (*vide* "The Pallavas," page 46,

Ch. IV, § VII) and of Vaikuntha Perumal at Kâñchîpuram.

It was probably Nandivarman Pallavamalla that built the temples of Muktêśvara (inscription No. 14 of 1893) and of Mataṇgêsvara (see Page 15 above) Kâñchîpuram.

The temple at Kûram was probably built in the 12th year of the reign of Dantivarman (No. 35 of 1900), a little before the year 800 and it must be remarked that this temple (vide *Pallava Architecture* by A. Rea, Plate CXXI), owing to its rearing lions, belongs also to the style of Râjasiṁha.

4° *The Style of Aparâjita.*

This style, which flourished in the second half of the IX century, is intermediate between the style of Râjasiṁha and that of the "Early Chôḷa."

The liṅgam is cylindrical; the sanctuary contains no image of Somaskanda; the Dvarapalakas have four arms; the kûdûs are surmounted with the head of a lion instead of the shovel-head of the ancient Pallava temples; there are no rearing lions at the base of the pillars. However, the corbels which are above the capitals have yet a circular profile and are exactly like those of the epoch of Râjasiṁha.

The monuments belonging to this period are very rare in Toṇḍai-maṇḍalam and, in spite of all the search we have made, we have been able to find but a single temple which certainly belongs to this period; it is the temple of Vîrattanêśvara that was built at Tiruttaṇi, during the reign of Aparâjita, the last of the Pallavas.